LONDON TRANSPORT

BUSES & COACHES

1961

LONDON TRANSPORT
BUSES & COACHES

1961

John A.S. Hambley

Published in 1997 by
Harold Martin & Redman Ltd

in conjunction with JOHN A.S. HAMBLEY
7 Linden Road,
Dunstable,
Beds. LU5 4NZ

Additional text and research by David A. Ruddom

British Library Cataloguing in Publication Data
A catalogue record for this book is available from the British Library

ISBN 1 901394 14 X

Front cover photograph:
Route 45, which had been born in the first stage of the tramway conversion in 1950, became part of the trolleybus conversion scheme during the year under review. It was extended daily from Farringdon Street to Hampstead Heath on 1st February in part replacement of trolleybus routes 513/613. Basically the route remained RTW operated, a Chalk Farm weekday allocation supplementing the existing Walworth duties. On Sundays Highgate garage was given three duties involving RMs more befitting a trolleybus replacement route although these only lasted until 25th April. RM388 is seen working one of these duties at South End Green, Hampstead Heath before departing on the rather tortuous journey to South Kensington Station. Unfortunately the rarity of this operation means that no one has observed that a 17 route blind is erroneously displayed and while three out of four points are correct, Highgate is certainly not. (Alan Mortimer)

Back cover photograph:
RF613, with the now customary orange perspex 'Pay As You Enter' slipboard fixed to the nearside, is working Route 473. The well laden bus, with still more travellers boarding, is seen in East Grinstead and, having commenced its journey at Crawley, only a short journey remains before its terminus at Dormansland is reached, a place name which is shown on contemporary maps as two words. (Alan Mortimer)

Designed by Hedgehog and produced by Hughes & Company, Kempsey, Worcestershire.
Printed and bound in Great Britain.

Nowadays the entrance to Harrow Weald garage provides the terminus for the 140 route to Heathrow which is worked from Hounslow but in 1961 it only saw buses on the route when they set out or arrived back on their duties from this garage. It was not until 1983 that the route swopped its Mill Hill section with 114. RT4629 leaves for work with an interesting array of vehicles inside the garage. RLH52 and 59 can be seen together with a number of RTs, while standing at the right somebody's pride and joy in the shape of a Rover car with fine wire spoked wheels partially obstructs the view of a GS class staff bus. This is probably either GS21 or GS78 both of which were allocated to HD at times during 1961. (Alan Mortimer)

Acknowledgements

This particular volume of London Transport Buses & Coaches, 1961, contains a large number of photographs from the cameras of several enthusiasts which have never before appeared in published book form. A big thank you is extended to all concerned for making this possible. As usual the source of the illustrations are individually acknowledged where known. Thanks are also due to those who have provided more accurate details of source on the few occasions in earlier volumes where credits have been wanting. A final thank you is extended to everyone who, in one way or another, has helped me publish this latest volume either by making photographs available or in providing information and advice in captioning the prints. These include Norman Anscomb, J.H.Aston, Bespix (Brian Speller), Dave Berwick, Terry Blois, C. Carter, D. Clark, Alan B.Cross, A.J.Douglas, John Gascoine, J.C.Gillham, Roger Holmes, L.G.Hooley, D.W.K.Jones, Kevin Lane, Mrs.B.Legg, Michael Lockyer, LPTS, Roy Marshall, J.H.Meredith, G.R.Mills, Alan Mortimer, A.D.Packet, Roger Partridge, Photobus, John H.Price, B.Rackman, Michael Rooum, D.Trevor Rowe, David A.Ruddom, R.H.G.Simpson, John Smith of Lens of Sutton, John G.S.Smith, Tom Smith, Ray Stanmore, R.E.Stevens, J.C.Walker, and Ron Wellings. Again factual information has been extracted from the various publications produced by the London Omnibus Traction Society, the Omnibus Society and the PSV Circle, the three leading organisations catering for the historian and enthusiast of road passenger transport in their respective spheres. David Ruddom and John G.S.Smith have assisted in many ways to bring this book to fruition and a special thank you is extended to them for all their help. Again on a personal note my wife Iris and David Ruddom's wife Enid must be mentioned for their support and understanding in the long hours of deliberation spent on this project by their spouses.

Publishers Note

As mentioned above many photographs in this volume have not previously been made available for others to enjoy. If you have prints or negatives stored away that have not previously been made generally available that might enhance future volumes then John Hambley would be pleased to hear from you.

Many of you have found the listing of photographs contained in this series of books which have been separately published by the author extremely useful. Unfortunately the amount of data has outgrown the capacity of the computer system on which it was being held and for the moment it will not be possible to continue this service. Copies of the listing in class or route number order covering the volumes 1939-45, 1946 and 1948-1956 are still available from the author at Dunstable, price £5.00 each. Please indicate whether you require class or route order.

Introduction

1961 proved to be a very busy year with regard to the changing means of road passenger transport within London. The programme of replacing trolleybuses by diesel powered motorbuses, which had commenced in 1959, continued throughout the year to leave just two more sizeable conversions needed to complete the changeover in the following year. A large number of new Central Area double deck bus routes was introduced, many of which were numbered in the once untouchable 200 series. With the more flexible nature of the motorbus the logical step was taken to extend or alter many former trolleybus services to enable more accessible and useful termini to be brought into use and also to integrate some of the established motorbus routes.

In the first ten months of the year other changes within the red bus sphere of operations were fairly minimal. The lowering of the road under the railway bridge at West Drayton allowed changes to be made on 15th March to the 204, 222 and 223 group of routes with a new 224C being introduced. New service 261, which opened up new roads to bus operation between New Barnet Station and Arnos Grove, commenced on 21st June. Of particular significance this year was the disappearance of the traditional Summer Sunday extensions of 93 to Dorking and 116 to Old Windsor, further evidence to prove the ascendancy of the private motor car. On 11th October a range of service changes took place including the loss of the Morden Underground Station circular route 156, which could be traced back to the 1926 Northern Line extension. In addition a programme of revisions took place to the trolleybus replacement routes in East London which had been introduced in the previous year.

The Country Area was to witness many small changes to services together with some withdrawals. The new towns had reached a levelling off in their development and changes in these areas were not so prolific as in some previous years. Most new routes introduced were variations of established routes giving a new suffixed number for the travelling public to worry about.

Road traffic conditions during the year worsened greatly with increasing car ownership. The programme of 'traffic management schemes' continued apace with many new one-way systems being introduced, sadly not always to the benefit of those using public transport with in many cases buses being denied access to the traffic objectives they were designed to serve. London Transport in its quest for better management of services extended the experimental Bus Electronic Scanning Equipment (BESI) already in use on Route 74 to cover in addition Routes 6, 13, 28, 31 and 73.

Athol Street, Poplar (C) garage, long associated with the Blackwall and Rotherhithe Tunnel routes, closed on the night of 10th/11th May, the staff, buses and duties being moved into the nearby Poplar (PR) garage which had been converted to bus operation in 1959. The reason for the delay was the provision of new staff facilities at Poplar.

Notable highlights during the year with regard to the bus and coach fleet were the arrival of the first Leyland engined Routemaster and the introduction of an unpainted example. RM632, delivered to the Executive in January with an AEC engine was almost immediately despatched first to Self Changing Gears in Coventry before moving on to the Leyland Works for the fitment of its 9.8 litre engine suitably modified for its operator's use. In an experiment aimed at future cost cutting RM664, known affectionately as the 'Silver Lady', took to the road during July finished in unpainted aluminium in similar style to the contemporary Underground rolling stock. It initially operated from Highgate but was eventually to see service from no fewer than eleven garages before being repainted into normal livery in 1965. Fortunately the tattiness of its later condition ruled out any adoption of this practice as far as buses were concerned.

RM8, which had first been shown at the Commercial Motor Exhibition held at Earls Court as long ago as 1958 was officially taken into stock. It had spent the intervening years in an experimental capacity which state oddly was to continue until eventually it was licensed for service in March 1976! The delivery of the first 30 feet long examples of the class took place towards the end of the year. The first three carried fleet numbers ER880 to ER882 but these were changed to RML before entry into service in Stage 12 of the trolleybus conversion programme. RML3 and CRL4 were similarly renumbered RM3 and RMC4 respectively during the year. The first continental visit to be made by a Routemaster occurred when RM546 journeyed to Basle, Rotterdam, The Hague and Paris.

The repainting of some Green Line coaches in the previous year into a paler green as the main body colour had proved unsuccessful and these coaches were restored to standard livery on overhaul or repaint. The three RW class buses purchased in the previous year to test the feasibility of one man operation of a dual door vehicle in the Country Area suffered three garage transfers during the year.

A summary of the changes to the road passenger fleet shows that new vehicles delivered, all in Central Area red livery, were made up entirely of the RM family and consisted of RM8, 600/17/24/25/32 - 879, 904 - 1030/32 - 71/73/74 and RML880 - 901. In the last month of the year British European Airways purchased a double deck Park Royal AEC Regent V registered 220CXK. London Transport of course continued to operate the London Airport coach service and maintain the vehicles on behalf of BEA and would have preferred the airline to buy Routemasters for double deck use. At this stage the cost involved led to this choice being made by the airline although in subsequent years Routemasters were bought. Against this total of 444 new vehicles delivered, 515 trolleybuses were disposed of together with 20 RTLs and 2 RTs plus one other, RT869, which was dismantled and scrapped. The only changes to the single deck fleet was the sale of ten GS buses which were the first of the class to be disposed of.

Many changes during the year are evident in the photographs and captions which follow, perhaps most notable being the introduction in November of via point blinds using upper and lower case lettering. One change recorded in the first Traffic Circulars of the year, which will not appear elsewhere in this volume, was the withdrawal of the farthing from legal tender. A loss of something from the past and the swinging sixties were just beginning!

Windsor garage received two of the new GS class vehicles in July 1954. Route 445 was converted from crew operated RF while Route 442, which had previously used an RT, was the other haunt of these OMO buses. GS77, being one of the original allocation, was to stay in passenger service until October 1962 when it was delicenced with no prospect of returning to revenue earning service with the Executive. The bus is seen in Windsor with behind it an early Austin badged Mini and a Ford Prefect while parked at the kerbside is a Vauxhall Wyvern or Velox of the original grille variety.

Elsewhere in this book you will find a picture of a bus on Route 81B displaying an 81A via points blind. Here, as RT430 heads homeward through Slough, the 81B display is being shown on an 81, ignoring Langley, Colnbrook and Harmondsworth. Although the Park Royal body carried and numbered 4827 which was first fitted on the chassis of RT1539 is of the most common variety it somehow doesn't look right with an HLX registration. The bus picks its way between a Morris Oxford and a post-war Ford Prefect in days before the Brunel Bus Station and the Wellington Street roundabout. (Photobus)

Emerging from Reform Street within the City of Dundee, ex-RT1483 rides over the disused tram tracks as it journeys to Grosvenor Road on Route 37. The retail premises on either corner have stood the test of time and their names are still familiar in many places today. It is pleasing to see that use has been made of the roof mounted number box which was so often removed from examples once they had left London although the other front apertures have been much rebuilt. (Ron Wellings)

Ex-RT1504 was purchased by Cunningham's Bus Services of Paisley in November 1957 from Bird's Commercial Motors who had acquired all the Craven bodied examples that were put up for sale by London Transport. With a background of grimy stone buildings in Paisley the bus is bound for the Renfrew Ferry terminus on the River Clyde. Since its service in London it has received a smart repaint and its roof route number box has been removed. Other London features such as the offside route number plate holder and duty running plate brackets are still in place. New fleet number 22 is now carried although later it was to be changed to 32. (Alan Mortimer)

Following the experiments in 1960 with the sixteen RF coaches on Route 711 and CRL4 using a lighter shade of green, some subsequent repaints appeared with the spare paint being used for relief colour on coaches which gave a rather darker appearance. It is difficult to tell on a black and white photograph but RF100, seen in Regent Street on its way to Godstone, looks as if it might be one such coach. (Ron Wellings)

Red Rover of Aylesbury's HLW218 was given fleet number 6 when it was purchased in September 1959 from Bird's of Stratford upon Avon. Once London Transport RT231 it is seen here in Kingsbury Square in its home town awaiting departure on the service to Westcott. Parked further along the road a 1958 built Bristol LD6B of United Counties, fleet number 539, waits to take up duties for a service to Luton on Route 16 - nowadays 61. The RT had first entered service from Croydon garage in November 1947 and between two overhauls and a small number of garage transfers was disposed of, still with its original Park Royal body, in July 1959. It remained in service with Red Rover until early 1965. (Ron Wellings)

The front roof dome of RT3194 shows the paint stripping carried out by continued contact with overhanging greenery. In use on Route 403 while garaged at Dunton Green it will receive its third overhaul in the following year and lose its down at heel appearance. Only the southern section details of the very long route are correctly shown in the via point blind box for the journey which will take it off route after Riverhead to run in to its home garage.
(Lens of Sutton)

Sevenoaks Bus Station provides the resting place for RF661 carrying DG5 running plates for its duty on Route 404 which used this terminus as the southern extreme of the route. In the 1949 book of this series T441 can be seen at the same location with the identical duty plates also waiting to depart for Shoreham Village which is situated half a mile off the A225 as it threads its way north to Dartford. Obviously this was a long standing duty. (D.Clark)

RT4522 in service on Route 441C, which was a daily service between Staines Central Station and Englefield Green, deviating in the latter place from the main 441 route to provide a service to Larchwood Drive. Only three lines of via point information are carried basically reflecting the short nature of the route, journey time on which was twenty three minutes. The display area for the new Austin A40 hiding within the shadows of this particular showroom almost looks purpose built but rather lacks illumination. (Ron Wellings)

Red Rover fleet number 1, ex-RT1475, is seen on 6th May in Aylesbury having just passed an AEC Reliance in the traditional City of Oxford livery. This Craven bodied RT, now minus its roof route number box had been initially disposed of by LTE to Bird's Commercial Motors in August 1956. After service with Red Rover and the associated Keith Coaches, the bus made a final journey back to the Stratford upon Avon dealer where in April 1965 it was noted partially scrapped. (Roger Partridge)

Green liveried RTL1285 waits on rain sodden St.Albans garage forecourt before departure on the full journey to Hertford Bus Station by way of Route 341. Despite this a short working blind for trips as far as Oaklands is displayed. Only one cyclist braves the adverse weather conditions in this wintry view of a corner of the City which still today looks much the same, although sadly the bus terminus and garage are no longer used. (Ron Wellings)

On 27th August TD54 stands at Kingston heading a queue of buses which includes RF388, TD118 and RF377. The delivery of these Central Area Mann Egerton bodied TDs was spread over nearly twelve months between 6th October 1948 and 30th September 1949. They were to continue in service until the last examples were withdrawn in October 1962, a process which had commenced in July 1958. This particular bus, still garaged at Kingston, was withdrawn from passenger service in December of the year under review to be used at varying times as a training vehicle until disposal in December 1963 to contractors in Blackshaw Road, Tooting called Durkin and Beeham Ltd. (Ralph E.Stevens)

RT634 is guaranteed longevity having gained a non-roofbox body at the time of overhaul in July 1960. By 1961 the policy of disposing of the earliest built chassis irrespective of the body carried had been superseded by the later plan of roofbox bodies being the deciding factor for sale regardless of the age of the chassis. Carrying an incorrect number blind, the bus is working from Slough to Farnham Road via Manor Park on Route 446A rather than 446. The clear use of the destination blind to show the variant intermediate point on this route, which only took 14 minutes journey time, probably renders the route number error a minor irrelevance. Indeed since the schedule required the conductor to change the route number every half an hour when Farnham Road was reached it was probably a very common error!

RT89 sits in Dartford Market while on learner duties in front of a service bus engaged on Route 96 on 6th May. Originally entering service in March 1941 from Putney Bridge garage and still carrying the same combination of chassis and body, the bus is now garaged at Stockwell. In a little over a year from now it would be disposed of to the Hamsters Mobile Theatre Group of East London as a replacement for their previously owned STD78, illustrated in the 1956 book of this series.
(Roger Partridge)

In the year under review disposal began of the little GS class of 26 seat normal control layout buses. GS40 and GS41 were the first to go in January being purchased by the West Bromwich Corporation Sports Department and in April the lower numbered moved on to the Health Department while GS41 was transferred to the passenger transport entity and was numbered 233. Here it stands at the West Bromwich garage in its new owner's colours with coat of arms and other inscriptions. Eventually this OMO bus became the property of the West Midlands PTE when that authority was formed in 1969, passing to a local dealer, Hudley, at Bilston for scrap in September 1972. (John Gascoine collection)

Traffic is busying up as RT3907 operating from Brixton garage makes its way to Purley along Brixton Hill on Route 109. This route 109 had appeared with the third post-war tram to bus conversion programme on 3rd April 1951 when fifty two RTs garaged at Brixton and thirty six from Thornton Heath took to the road to replace tram services 16 and 18. At that time it was London's most frequent bus route with sixty four buses an hour scheduled in one peak hour spell on the section between Kennington and Brixton. (Alan Mortimer)

After its sale by the Executive in February 1953, ex-B15 was operated in passenger service by the Lincolnshire Road Car Company of Lincoln, firstly as their fleet number 983 and then renumbered 2108 in November 1953. Withdrawn from service in November 1960 it was converted to a tree cutter receiving service fleet number 9. Still with its original body structure neatly converted it now awaits the call to attend to some overhanging foliage or obstruction. (Ron Wellings)

In the 1951 book of this series, single deck LT1123 negotiates this once famous landmark at the top of Summer Hill, Chislehurst. On 23rd September of the year now under review a much younger RF352 emerges from the arch as it journeys to Penge, Crooked Billet on Route 227. Some minor changes to the background are noticeable in the wicker work fencing which has been added behind the ageing metal railings to the left of the picture and in the fast growing greenery on the right of which there was no sign in the earlier picture. (Roger Partridge)

Former C111 is admired by an appreciative audience on 24th September outside the Beulah Spa Hotel at Upper Norwood, having been acquired by the Vintage Passenger Vehicle Association of London a few months earlier. Still wearing the London Fire Brigade colours, though with its previous owner's insignia removed, work on restoration appears to have already begun. All followers of the preservation scene will know that this Interstation Leyland Cub, since returned to its original sky blue and cream livery, is now owned by Alan Cross and is in fairly regular attendance at rallies some thirty six years on. (Bespix)

RTL1537, pictured on 22nd October at the Roehampton terminus of Route 30, appears to have an identity problem, although it must be added that this was a fairly rare occurrence in the huge fleet of road vehicles operated by London Transport. It is carrying the registration number of RTL1617 instead of its correct OLD646. It had earlier in the month been returned to service from its second visit to Aldenham Works for overhaul being outshopped with body number 9080 which had first seen use on the chassis of RTL1510. Presumably the error was soon corrected. A new water can appears to have recently been provided which sits quite happily unprotected alongside the bus stop. (John Gascoine)

Standing at the Archway terminus of Route 27, RT2686 still carries a body of Weymann construction although it received this particular roof box example in August 1959 on the occasion of its second overhaul. With the policy adopted by the Executive in the early 1960s of disposing of this type of body it said good bye to London in October 1964. It was exported to South Africa to be operated by Cape Electric Tramways of Cape Town. Here the Holloway crew take their ease before undertaking the three and a quarter hours round trip to Teddington. (Alan Mortimer)

Elmers End garage became involved with Route 64 on a daily basis at the time of the seventh stage of the trolleybus conversion on 20th July 1960 and received a small allocation of RMs for the purpose. RM275 is seen in Croydon as it journeys to Tooting Broadway which became the terminus on 9th May when the route was cut back from Wimbledon Stadium. The extension to this point had only been introduced because of the lack of a suitable terminus in Tooting at the time. (Alan Mortimer)

The first of the year's trolleybus abandonment schemes took place on 1st February and among the array of extended or new routes introduced was the resurrection of route number 17 which replaced trolleybus routes 517 and 617. This route number had lain dormant since 1958 when it ceased operation between London Bridge and Shepherds Bush. The new route traversed the roads between North Finchley and Farringdon Street via Grays Inn Road on Mondays to Saturdays, continuing on to Camberwell Green Mondays to Fridays. Here on 11th July RM595, one of the initial allocation of 117 RMs to Highgate to cover for their involvement in stage 9 of the electric to diesel programme sits beneath the trolleybus wiring at North Finchley before departure to the City. (J.H.Aston)

The author doesn't particularly recall this 'Collectors' Corner' which appears to be all that remained of a wartime incident but it looks as though it might have been an interesting place to visit. The three pedestrians have taken the advice painted on the roadway to look right as RTW315 passes on its way to Pimlico on Route 24. First entering service in May 1950 at Barking, three overhauls later finds it operating from Chalk Farm and it remained the property of London Transport until disposed of in December 1966 for further work in Ceylon. (M.Rooum)

On 24th June at Crystal Palace Parade RF4 is seen in use on a private bus service to the Construction Equipment Exhibition being held at Crystal Palace between 15th and 24th June. The rather attractive and professionally produced route blind is complemented by paper stickers added to some windows while the concertina blinds on the coving windows are all drawn suggesting this was a hot sunny day. Originally entering service in May 1951 this RF first operated from Streatham and although it made many garage transfers during its operational life it returned quite often to AK as here. It was back at Streatham when withdrawn in September 1963. Disposed of to Passenger Vehicle Sales of Ilford in December 1963 it had a chequered career until moving into preservation in January 1979. (John H.Meredith)

Green liveried RTL1285 lays over at New Barnet Station before commencing another journey to Hitchin by way of Route 303A. In 1959 in a change of policy eighteen RTLs were painted green to provide needed additional vehicles in the Country Area. However, it was July 1960 before agreement was reached with the Unions and the Country Area that they could be used in this sphere of operation. Even then, the staff of Hatfield garage, who were given the Leylands, complained bitterly and in June of the year under review they were replaced by newly overhauled former Central Area RTs. (Ron Wellings)

Ex-T506 in the ownership of Jones & Stephany of London, N16 as a mobile furniture showroom now shows wear in its latest role. It had been initially disposed of to W.North of Leeds in May 1954 and after successful negotiations was soon to be seen again in London and further afield. It rather looks as if at sometime it had been involved in a mishap with newly repainted lower offside panelling to the cab. It was to pass to Wood & Lambert in December, another organisation from the same area of London for uncertain use and from which it seems to have disappeared without trace. (R.F.Mack)

On 15th February, having just returned from its overhaul earlier in the month, RT4576 shows off the fine craftsmanship of the Aldenham Works as it stands on the roadway of Abbey Wood garage. This particular bus will be well remembered by many enthusiasts many years later when as a publicity vehicle it was used by Capital Radio with a partially rebuilt upper deck which retained its front portion but was open top at the rear half. Although sold for preservation in July 1983 it does not appear on any contemporary lists of such vehicles. (Roger Partridge)

Many photographs throughout this series of books have included this long standing brickwork at Watford Junction by the side of buses and in this case it is RT3529 and RF698. No doubt it will be included in many more since it still stands to this day although nowadays vehicles use a purpose built interchange facility immediately opposite. The bus, a normal resident of Two Waters garage, carries TG4 for its duty on Route 301 to Aylesbury passing both of these garages on its journey. Body number 7710 is now carried since its return to service from its April 1960 overhaul, being of the same basic RT8 type fitted when new. RF698 (NLE647) in use on Route 322 awaits departure for Hemel Hempstead using the same roads as the 301 until diverging at Hunton Bridge to use minor roads to the east of the Grand Union Canal to reach its destination. (Roger Partridge)

After its opening in 1956 the area immediately beside Hemel Hempstead bus station was quickly developed and The Great Harry public house was added to the new town skyline. GS83 had first entered service in December 1954 after nearly twelve months in storage and after revenue earning use at Crawley, Dorking and Hemel Hempstead was delicensed in October 1962. It was then stored within Garston garage until sold in December 1963. Here it works the 316 route, jointly operated with the Rover Bus Service. (Ron Wellings)

At Station Place, Finsbury Park with the girders of the abortive Northern City Line extension still in place, Holloway garaged RT1395 waits departure on weekdays Route 4 to Surrey Docks Station now called Surrey Quays in keeping with its more up-market image. This bus would be disposed of with the body seen here numbered 1687 in October 1963 to commence another lengthy and varied life. First acquired by Albert's Coaches of London E9, it moved on through the following years with such well known organisations as Lesney Products Ltd., PVS of Upminster, then the Executors of Samuel Ledgard and later on to the West Yorkshire Road Car Company. It moved back to PVS, by then of Canvey Island, and later to Isleworth Coaches before being scrapped by Autobreakers of Isleworth in June 1969. A distinguished career for a bus which first entered service in August 1950. (Alan Mortimer)

Deserted Plumstead Common in the depths of winter provides the background for RT3477 as it heads for Plumstead Garage on the Sunday extension of Route 53 which on a full working at this time reached Erith. For many years the Plumstead Garage terminal was described on destination blinds as Bostall Woods which could be reached by a short walk for the garage. This RT from New Cross is carrying an earlier roofbox body. (Alan Mortimer)

TD87 has only around another twelve months in the ownership of the Executive before its departure to the Mayflower Family Centre of Canning Town in June 1962. Delivered to London Transport and first entering service from Muswell Hill garage in April 1949, the bus received two overhauls. Within this batch of one hundred vehicles only two ever swopped bodies and so this bus carries the same body with which it subsequently operated at Leyton and North Street, Romford before arriving at Kingston in August 1959. This was to prove to be its last operational base, being withdrawn from service in March 1962. The wood framed bodywork of the 1/1TD2 buses originally seated 31 passengers but between July and October 1954 all were reduced to 30 seats by the removal of the double seat opposite the front entrance. The single replacement provided a space for the conductor to stand and avoid his feet being trampled on. This is Esher and the shops include a branch of the then well known dry cleaners Achille Serre. (Alan Mortimer)

Route number 214 had lain dormant since 29th October 1941 when the Kingston to Walton operation was double decked and renumbered 131. Times and circumstances having changed, new route 214 was introduced on 1st February of the year under review replacing the 615 trolleybuses with double deck RM motor buses from Highgate garage between Parliament Hill Fields and Moorgate, where this picture of RM586 was taken on 11th November. With the removal of the buildings behind the RMs, ghostly fireplaces on the facing wall remind one of earlier warmth in days before central heating. (John Gascoine)

Having journeyed up from Bromley garage RF457 now finds itself in the unfamiliar surroundings of the side roads around Dalston garage while waiting to complete its transfer to its new abode. Did the staff at its former garage decide this particular RF should be the one to move to save them the bother of replacing one of the quarter drop windows? Route blinds will have to be fitted while the TB garage code painted on the side and crudely chalked through will also need attention before the bus can re-enter service. (John Gascoine)

Ex-RT1500 in splendid repainted condition makes full use of the London Transport route box apertures as it operates for its new owners, Longstaff of Mirfield on their Route 11 to Dewsbury via Knowl. This Craven bodied RT had initially entered Central Area service in November 1949 but received a Country Area livery in May 1956, eleven months before disposal to Bird's Commercial Motors in April 1957. As with so many of these earliest disposals of the post-war RT class, it only lasted a comparatively short number of years with its new owners and in June 1963 it was noted at W.North's premises awaiting scrapping. (Norman Anscomb collection)

H & C Transport of Watford could be contacted on a couple of Garston telephone numbers given on the blind should you require to hire this bus which was originally RT221. It had been acquired in March 1959 and saw service until being withdrawn in January 1968 eventually being reduced for scrap after arriving at the Goldthorpe, South Yorkshire premises of a dealer called Johnson in June of that year. Originally entering service in the first year of post-war RT operation it carried body number 1470, built by Park Royal with a route number roof box. It still carries this same body although the roof box has been removed. The London Transport fleet number is surprisingly retained on the cab panelling. The bus is seen here beneath the trolleybus wires of North West London with a few passengers probably on a work's contract. (Norman Anscomb collection)

The entrance to St.Albans Abbey Station displays an old style British Railways sign on 7th March as RT4050 passes on its way to Maple Cross. The bus carries Luton garage plates although it is actually a Garston bus. It has always been in Country Area livery since it initially entered service in 1951, being the last of a batch of twenty bodied by Weymann whose next green batch commenced at RT4099. (Roger Partridge)

RT4170 turns into Pier Road, Gravesend while in use on the works service Route 495A between Rosherville down by the Thames and Christianfields Estate. Nowadays no routes deviate down to the river at this point. This particular RT fleet number survived with London Transport from its introduction in June 1951 right through to October 1978. (Ron Wellings)

RF394 arrived at Hounslow garage upon return to service from its second overhaul in January of the year under review having previously spent its earlier years at Sutton. It travels under the trolleybus wiring for Route 657 which accompanied it out of Hounslow as far as Wellington Road. The unusual use of the hoardings behind is interesting with the Bisto kid apparently climbing on to the roof of the RF. (Alan Mortimer)

In the first month of the year under review the three members of the RW class were transferred to Addlestone from their previous operational base at Two Waters, Hemel Hempstead. They were put to work chiefly on three routes: the 427, 437 and 456, which each followed slightly different routes between Weybridge and Woking. RW2 as WY1 passes the 'White Hart' at New Haw on Route 437 as it journeys to Woking with a respectable number of passengers. (Alan Mortimer)

Climbing the short Traps Lane before reaching the summit of the small hill and turning into Coombe Lane on its journey to Kingston, RF349 carries a small number of passengers not exactly taxing the work load of the conductor who can be seen doubtless conversing with his driver. The only alteration which has been made to the vehicle since it first entered service towards the end of 1952 is the addition of trafficators. The image is a little tarnished by the painted on garage code and the advertising now carried at roof level. (Alan Mortimer)

To avoid waiting delivery of new buses after they had elected to abandon the remaining tramway system, Dundee Corporation Department acquired thirty Craven bodied London Transport RTs in 1956. On 7th October ex-RT1454, now Dundee 214, operates on route 37 at Nethergate, running over unused tram tracks which present a nasty hazard to the scooter rider in front. There is no sign of overhead wiring which by now had been removed. The atmosphere of a provincial city going about its daily business is well portrayed in this long shot which includes many interesting stone built buildings. (J.H.Price)

The Atomic Energy Research Establishment acquired a number of ex-G class buses in the early 1950s which included G169. This NCME bodied Guy Arab II had entered service with London Transport in July 1945 having been delivered in a brown and cream livery with wooden slatted seating. In August 1948 the seating was upgraded to moquette and a year later a repaint into the more usual livery was carried out. After operation first from Alperton and later Barking garages the bus was disposed of to the Ministry of Supply in May 1952 where it was to give ten further years service transporting employees engaged on this highly secretive form of energy. J.Lloyd & Sons of Nuneaton operated the bus for a further year still basically in the condition in which it left London and in 1963 it was part-exchanged with Arlington Motors for a second-hand RT and scrapped. (Surfleet Transport Photographs)

Hounslow bus station with a number of buses including two RTs awaiting departure on short workings on Routes 116 and 117. On the left RT684, will be leaving for a journey as far as Bedfont Green, about half the full length of the route to Staines. On the right RT2058 will only reach Lower Feltham before returning on duty AV15. (Ron Wellings)

The RMs which worked on Sundays on trolleybus route 609 tended to operate short journeys between North Finchley and Islington Green and RM586 is doing this as it arrives at the foot of Archway Road by the Whittington College. Unfortunately in later years this pleasant greenery was swept away by road widening. The skate on the trolleybus wiring above the bus sent a signal to the interval recording clock in the foyer at 55 Broadway, the set of which were always a source of fascination in those days. Routemaster operation on the trolleybus route of course made the system somewhat inaccurate on Sundays in its latter days.

Dundee Corporation Transport HGC224, once STL2691, with redesigned blind boxes is in use on Route 35 having arrived at the City Centre on 25th September, the Corporation Transport clock giving the time as 12.15. New operators were immediately found by North's, the Leeds dealer, for the complete batch of nine year old Weymann bodied AEC Regents when disposed of by London Transport in July and August 1955. The livery worn by Dundee's examples was green with white relief between decks but by the end of the year under review the white was discarded, resulting in a rather drab and much criticised appearance. (A.J.Douglas)

Park Royal bodied ex-G151 with rebuilt front blind apertures is seen while in the ownership of W.Alexander and Sons of Falkirk carrying fleet number RO699. Unfortunately the photographer can no longer recall the precise location of this picture but the garage code P may well indicate Perth and 'Mill Street 110' may mean something to one of our Scots readers. (Ron Wellings)

RF13 was often garaged at Merton for varying lengths of time during its twelve plus years with the Executive. Now wearing the drab all over dark green livery for its use on private hire workings it is seen leaving an unusually quiet Wembley sports complex. Unfortunately all these private hire coaches were withdrawn from service between June 1962 and November 1963. Thankfully this is now another example of a preserved vehicle after having completed many years service with Hampson's Luxury Coaches Ltd. of Oswestry. (R.H.G.Simpson)

GS6 waits at Oxted for a short working journey to Chart Church by way of Route 464 on 21st October. This route was interworked with others in the area around Oxted and during the course of a day a particular bus could be seen on a number of different routes. After a passenger service career spent almost entirely at Chelsham garage save for a very short period in 1962 at Dorking, this bus was disposed of to the Rank Organisation in July 1963. (John H.Meredith)

With the closure of Athol Street garage on 10th May its entire stock of fifty two RTLs was moved into nearby Poplar garage along with two of their three RFWs, the third moving on to Camberwell. Since its first involvement with the diesel bus on 11th November 1959, Poplar had only operated RM class vehicles but as this picture taken on 17th June shows both RM and RTL class vehicles are now in abundance. RTL535, the subject of the photograph, has its loosely fitted front blind set for the Special Dock Service between Custom House and Manor Way which PR inherited in the change. To the right and in the background can be seen RM22 with next to it an unknown RTL and RTL1051 dressed for Route 108A. (John Gascoine)

On 17th June Poplar garaged RTL424 and RTL389 wait their respective departure times from Bromley by Bow while in use on Route 108A to Eltham, Southend Crescent. Both buses had been previously housed at Athol Street garage which had long been associated with the Blackwall and Rotherhithe Tunnel routes. The closure of this garage on 10th May was later than originally intended due to the need to provide new canteen facilities in the area which were not ready until this date. (John Gascoine)

Viewed passing through Hammersmith on Route 716A to Woking, RF247 for some reason lacks the customary side route board which would have given more detail of places served than the front blind manages. Route 716A came about on 5th October 1955 by diverting the most northerly part of the then service 717 at Valley Road Corner to journey on to Stevenage. With the present public transport situation a similar trip by road between the towns at either end of this route would entail a very arduous trek. (Alan Mortimer)

The first GS disposals were made during the year under review when ten examples, having been unlicenced for varying periods of time, were found buyers. Additionally two further members saw work as staff buses, adding to a small number which had been used in this capacity. GS44 was one of these new recruits and was allocated to Abbey Wood followed in turn by New Cross garage. Eventually it returned to passenger use and was to see service from Epping, Dorking and Hertford, before storage at Hatfield for some eighteen months and final sale in March 1968. With some seats remaining unused the bus leaves Fulwell trolleybus depot within which can be seen BEA 4RF4 type airport coaches. A post-war Ford Anglia bounces across the depot tram rails which had been last used in pre-war days. (Michael Rooum)

Buses on Route 156 had always been associated with Morden Underground station since its opening in 1926 when the route commenced as a feeder service from Cheam. On 11th October in the year under review the route was sadly withdrawn in a major revision of routes in the area. Standing within the Morden station forecourt RT2917 nearest the camera and RT2664 reveal on their destination blinds the circular nature of the route in its final days. (Ron Wellings)

The trolleybus wiring at the Smithfield terminus in St.John Street will still be required for another four days for the 679 route but Clapton's RTL1591 is working the 277 route which replaced the erstwhile 677 trolleybus some two years earlier. The RTL had a comparatively short existence at Clapton garage being transferred in during April 1960 and moving on to Aldenham Works for its first overhaul in December 1961. (John H.Meredith)

Some sort of oil leak appeared to be giving the offside front wheel assembly fitted to RTL1036 a problem when it was photographed inside Poplar garage on 11th February. The Wanstead Flats destination is nothing to do with Route 82, being intended for Route 40 although RTL1489 parked further inside the building has the correct Rotherhithe display associated with Route 82. (John Gascoine)

RT1834 received an overhaul in August 1958 whereupon it was outshopped from Aldenham carrying Saunders built body number 7378 to re-enter service from Holloway garage, a bastion of this class. It had previously been a long time resident of Elmers End, albeit with a different manufacturer's bodywork. In use on Route 27 in July it is seen making its way along Kensington Church Street heading for its summer weekend terminus at Hampton Court. Although the sun shines at twelve minutes past one the bus carries few passengers on the cross town venture to this well patronised tourist attraction. (Tom Smith)

RT3538 managed two overhauls, the first in February 1956 and the second in January 1960 when it was outshopped with this Park Royal body, number 2008. Here it journeys to Grove Park on Route 36B managed by a Rye Lane garage crew. January 1963 saw the bus transferred to its final operating garage of Wood Green before being unlicensed to await disposal, which took place in October 1964 when it left for the dealer, Don Everall of Wolverhampton. Solid and apparently well kept dwellings form the background to this New Cross picture but car ownership in future years would present a problem. (Alan Mortimer)

RF179 was delivered to Dorking garage in March 1952, Epping being only the second establishment to operate the coach and it is seen here at the Bus and Coach Station, Aldgate in unblemished condition laying over on Route 720 before departure to Bishops Stortford. (Alan Mortimer)

The Hackney garage driver of RTL1312 has decided to disregard the 'No Parking' notice and leave his bus in the fashion which pedestrians regard as intolerable. This view of Clapton garage is interesting as conduit tram track can be seen still in place from the days when this was Hackney tram depot. Tram operation ceased here on 4th November 1939 in favour of trolleybuses which in due course gave way to motor buses on 14th April 1959. In 1950, while still a trolleybus depot, the name was changed from Hackney to Clapton to avoid confusion with the nearby bus garage of the same name and which is the home of the RTL which has turned short on Route 30 on the 17th June. The destination 'Hackney Station' was itself a peculiarity, the station to which it refers having finally closed in 1945. (John Gascoine)

Finally disposed of in April 1964 following a career of serving Londoners for nearly seventeen years, RT429 still carries an RT3 type body after three overhauls. It is seen at Hounslow bus station in what can only be described as poor weather conditions with snow falling to make driving conditions even more hazardous when departure time arrives for the journey as AV1 on Route 110 to Twickenham Station. (Alan Mortimer)

West Green garaged RTL599 at Turnpike Lane Station emerges from Westbury Avenue on Sunday 20th August as it makes its way to Alexandra Park, Victoria on Route 231. The number had been resurrected in May 1954 when Route 144B was renumbered. Trolleybus wiring is still in evidence for the 521, 621 and 641 routes which were still running at this time and on the right wires emerge from Turnpike Lane Bus Station for journeys which have turned short from the south, usually on the 641. (Roger Partridge)

With running duty plates WH300, RM459 stands at Stratford Broadway, driver and conductor ready for the off on Route 41 to Highgate, Archway Station. This was the first route to receive the eight feet wide RTW type buses and in Stage 6 of the trolleybus conversion programme on 27th April 1960, the weekday extension to Stratford added help to the Tottenham RTWs with Routemasters from West Ham garage. The Sunday route remained Archway and Tottenham Hale and for a time Holloway (J) garage assisted on that day. (Roger Partridge)

RT4562 was soon to lose its Central Area colours when in June it reappeared from overhaul in Country Area green. Here, still in its red livery, it performs as T2 on Route 144 and is seen journeying to Turnpike Lane Station at South Woodford. Since its introduction to the rigours of service in London during December 1953 the bus first saw service from Sutton before moving to its present home but when painted green would move to Hemel Hempstead. The driver and several of the passengers are obviously distracted by the photographer on his lofty perch.
(Alan Mortimer)

GS20, now garaged at Hertford for the second time, is seen while in use on Route 333 on which certain journeys still operated beyond the confines of Hertford town to the little hamlet of Chapmore End. The 333 first used this type of bus from November 1953 when they took over from the outgoing C class. On 30th October 1957 the three GSs then allocated were replaced by two OMO operated RFs but with interworkings the smaller buses reappeared in the early 60s and were to last until the end of GS operation at Hertford on 22nd November 1968. Interestingly the number 333 has recently been restored to the Hertford town service. (Ron Wellings)

Epping Station, one of the most unlikely outposts of the 'tube', served by the Central Line, provides the background for RT4516 which is somewhat inconsiderately parked. The 396 service to Bishops Stortford commenced either at the garage or the station in Epping and with not a passenger in sight the latter seems probable in this particular instance. A Hillman Minx Series II estate and a Ford Prefect car are parked on the station approach. This fleet number had been in use for exactly twenty years when in May 1974 the then current combination of chassis and body were sold to Wombwell Diesels for scrap. (Ron Wellings)

Standing at the Chiswick terminus of Route 55, Southall garaged RT2114 waits its departure for Hayes, Bourne Avenue. The little girl is more interested in the goings on at the platform than the photographer which her guardian is trying to point out to her. Both advertisements carried by the bus are slightly ambiguous - how on earth do the promoters know all that they say is true? When this bus was finally disposed of by London Transport in August 1976, a Monsieur Wisebecker of Bonneuil, France became the new owner. (Alan Mortimer)

Cunningham's Bus Service of Paisley has repainted ex-RT213 into a very attractive livery reminiscent in a black and white photograph of the earlier colour scheme worn by London Transport vehicles. This Park Royal bodied bus only ever operated from Potters Bar garage having been placed in service during November 1947 as part of the batch to replace open staircase LT class buses on Route 134. After two overhauls at October 1951 and March 1955 it was withdrawn from service and moved to temporary store at Stockwell and then disposed of to Bird's during the month of December 1958. Several early disposals of RTs were made where no body changes had taken place and this RT still carries its original body, number 1462, albeit now minus the roofbox. It is seen at Paisley on 19th May. (A.J.Douglas)

This broadside view of RTW147 gives no indication of its additional six inches width. The conductor, who appears to be one of 'the old school', complete with his Gibson ticket machine, wisely grips the upright stanchion as the bus makes the right hand turn at Stoke Newington Common on 13th June. The RTW has worked short on Route 76 and carries running number AR7. (John Gascoine)

Ruislip Station Approach is the resting place for RT2495 before commencement of a further run to Brentford, Half Acre on Route 97. Southall garage had taken custody of this RT in December 1958 when it was returned to service with body number 1935 first carried by RT656. This was its second and last overhaul and in May 1964 Acrow (Engineers) of London were to become the new owners. The pleasant 1904 Ruislip Station buildings, the LGOC bus stop post, albeit with a modern flag, give a period flavour to the picture. (Ron Wellings)

RT643 had a fairly short career with London Transport confining itself to operating from a variety of northern area country garages. First entering service in September 1948 from Grays garage it was housed at Harlow in December 1963 when it was delicensed to be disposed of in May 1964 to the Ceylon Transport Board. It is seen here carrying body number 2267, which was first mounted on RT988, resting at the bus and coach station at Aldgate before returning to Harlow Bus Station on a 720A relief journey. RF228 is the only other vehicle that can be identified and that waits to take up duties to Bishops Stortford on Route 720. The driver would appear to be giving the inspector a piece of his mind on some matter. (Kevin Lane)

When Hanwell became a bus garage they initially remained locked on to their former wirebound routes but in the summer programme of 1961 they received five Sunday duties on Route 97 to support Southall who of course worked RTs. Here RM469 heads down Bury Street, Ruislip bound for Brentford on one of these duties. Delivered to London Transport in September 1960 it was immediately placed in store at Hounslow until its passenger operating career commenced in November of that year. (Alan Mortimer)

This rear end view of T219 standing within the embryonic Clapham Transport Museum shows work in progress for the eventual opening to the general public. The coach actually entered service at Romford garage in January 1931. Some examples of the same type had started their careers the previous month at Slough and so the panel in the offside window is correct in stating '1930 Green Line coach T class'. A Metropolitan stage carriage plate, number 410, has been faithfully replaced and the only modern fitments are the circular reflector units to meet the needs of contemporary road use. (D.W.K.Jones)

This posed view at Finchley depot shows the changing scene brought about by stage twelve of the trolleybus conversion. From left to right 1951 built RT2616 is working Muswell Hill's long standing commitment on route 125 which was to come to an end when the route transferred to Finchley on 8th November. Trolleybus 1488, an L3 class vehicle dating from June 1940 is blinded for the 609 trolleybus route which was to be replaced by bus route 104 using the new 30 feet long variety of Routemaster as represented by RML880, the first of the class. (Alan Mortimer)

With the twelfth stage of the trolleybus conversion programme Londoners were introduced to the first use of upper and lower case lettering on via point blinds. Holloway, Finchley, New Cross and Wood Green garages started using them from 8th November with their involvement on routes 4A, 104, 125, 141, 141A, 168, 221, 259 and 269. RM649 operating from WN garage shows off the new style while negotiating the crossroads immediately outside Wood Green Underground station. This RM had entered service in April with the tenth stage of the changeover having been in store previously at Loughton garage since delivery in January. (Alan Mortimer)

The first sales of the GS class took place during the year under review with the demise of GSs 24, 32, 37, 40, 41, 43, 49, 61, 63 and 70, ten in total, of which it is known at least two still survive in preservation. GS70 however is not one of the two. On 22nd July it stands in the livery of its new owners the West Ham Borough Handicapped Persons Voluntary Welfare Committee who fitted it with rear doors and a tail lift. A comparatively short history with London Transport had commenced on 18th December 1953 when in company with three others of the class it was delivered to the Executive from the bodybuilders Eastern Coach Works of Lowestoft. Entering service from Tring garage in January 1954 it was then transferred to Garston in July 1956, received an overhaul in December 1957 and re-entered service again from Garston. In September 1958 it went on long term hire to Great Yarmouth Corporation and on its return in July 1959 was put into store in the basement of Victoria garage. Further storage at Grays and Romford, London Road followed culminating in its sale in April of the year under review. (W.R.Legg)

A 1953 built Country Area bus together with an early post-war Maidstone and District Bristol journey along New Road, Gravesend on 3rd May. RF659 had been converted for OMO with the loss of two passenger seats in July 1958 and now with the prominent orange perspex 'Pay As You Enter' sign carried below the nearside front window has just commenced its journey on Route 489A to Meopham, Hook Green. A motley collection of buildings form the background, typical of Gravesend in the early sixties. The Salvation Army citadel frontage could almost date from the 1865 period of the founding of this Christian movement but the added sales area in front now provides a men's tailoring outlet. (Roger Partridge)

RTL675 waits beneath the trees at Highbury Barn on 13th June to return south on the route 19 service to Tooting Bec Station. Redevelopment work had caused the time honoured stand in Kelvin Road to be moved to here on the opposite side of Highbury Grove down which an RF scuttles in the background on Route 236. This well travelled RTL, which first entered service in February 1950, is now eight months away from receiving its third overhaul and currently carries body number 4025 with which it was outshopped from Aldenham in January 1958.
(John Gascoine)

Originally G298, an NCME bodied Guy Arab II which first entered service with London Transport during December 1945, the bus soldiers on with W.Alexander & Sons of Falkirk in this view taken in Perth in January of the year under review. Later in the year the decision was taken to divide the Alexander fleet into three separate companies based upon the existing northern, southern and Fife operating areas. The southern area was entitled Alexander & Sons (Midland) Ltd. and R0712 was then operated for several months as MR0712 until eventual disposal which came in 1962. (Ray Stanmore)

Riverside garaged RTL790 is in the last stage of its journey on Route 72 to Esher as it passes along Hook Rise South paralleling the Kingston By Pass. The flag on the lamp standard denotes a compulsory bus stop but a request stop only for Green Line route 715. These combination stops could be very colourful affairs. The slipboard carried announces that at its northern end the route passed the famous White City Stadium, now only a memory. (Ron Wellings)

On 25th August two ex-STD class buses are seen in Sarajevo, Yugoslavia with reversed platforms to cope with driving on the right. Both vehicles' registrations, 6X749 and 6X2181 are clear but their respective London fleet numbers are not known at present. While the blind boxes have been panelled over the roof route number boxes remain in place thereby retaining their unmistakable London image. (D.Trevor Rowe)

Travelling through the Blackwall Tunnel had always been likely to involve delays and in order to alleviate these irregularities Route 108B had been introduced in October 1960 to serve just the southern section on Mondays to Fridays between the Star in the East at Greenwich and Crystal Palace. Catford worked this route and their RT795 runs past the impressive building of the Greenwich Town Social Club. (Ron Wellings)

On 11th March deserted RT701 operating from Uxbridge garage stands at Uxbridge Station, halfway point of Route 223 from Ruislip to West Drayton Station. This is just four days before restructuring of the 222/223/224 group of routes and changes to the 204 which were made possible by the completion of work to lower the road under the railway bridge at West Drayton. From the 15th of the month Route 223 was extended to operate daily from Ruislip to Hounslow Garage. (Ron Wellings)

Now with a background completely alien to that it had known when owned by London Transport, ex-RTL8 rides the rolling countryside of South Wales between Carmarthen and Llanelly with what appears to be a good load of passengers. Built in 1949 this bus has been pictured twice previously in this series of books while in London service at Tooting and Upton Park. (Alan Mortimer)

RF591, having minutes earlier commenced service from the Church Green terminus at Harpenden, now turns off the main A6 road to pass the railway station on its journey via Batford, Wheathampstead, St.Albans and Radlett to Borehamwood on Route 355. Harpenden has escaped the attention of developers in the main to this present day unlike some other parts of Hertfordshire and although the vehicles have long since been replaced, an exact comparison photograph can be taken today although with the inevitable traffic island in the foreground. (Alan Mortimer)

Three Green Line reliefs, the first two being Northfleet vehicles for Route 701 while the furthest operates from Dunton Green garage on Route 705, await their recall for use parked at New Cross garage on 6th December. Presumably the Christmas present buying spree has involved the use on this Wednesday of, from left to right, RT3612, RT620 and RT3624. All three carry Green Line fleet names although RT620 lacks the between decks motif. (John Gascoine)

West Green garage was the second garage to receive RTLs and remained faithful to the class until the last week or so before the garage closed in January 1962 when RTs were moved in preparatory to Wood Green taking over their operations. They also operated five RMs between April and November of the year under review as a temporary measure to assist Wood Green during its dual motorbus/trolleybus existence. The driver of RTL1279 in Westbury Avenue has either already changed or maybe not bothered to change the Edmonton destination as he heads towards Turnpike Lane on the short working shuttle on 144 which later became satellite route W1. (Alan Mortimer)

57

These two buses passing through Harpenden should be ten minutes apart and the Watford destination of the leading vehicle, RT3608, suggests it may have been seriously delayed. RT4793 on the 321A has probably only started from Church Green at Harpenden while the 321 will have worked through from Luton. The 321A is destined for Rickmansworth, Tudor Way which name was introduced on 25th October to differentiate this turning point from the new Berry Lane Estate terminus further on which was reached from that date by buses on 385/385A. (Alan Mortimer)

Red liveried RT4630 has only a few months to continue in service operating from Hounslow garage where it stands before it was to enter Aldenham works for overhaul to be outshopped in green livery. Eighteen RTs during the year were to make this transformation from Central to Country Area use with the decision to withdraw the only green liveried RTLs which had seen service at Hatfield garage for less than a year. Standing just inside the garage is RT596 now with an RT8 body. As delivered RT596 had the distinction of being numerically the last red RT before the first batch of Country Area examples appeared with RT597 entering service at Tring garage in July 1948. (Alan Mortimer)

RT4700 took on a completely different aspect when in May of the year under review it re-emerged from its second overhaul at Aldenham in Country Area livery. Being put into service at Hatfield, it would no longer suffer the stresses of rumbling over road surfaces of the type clearly seen here glistening in the wet conditions. Officially garaged at Upton Park from new in February 1954 it was to receive its first overhaul and be returned to service at Leyton in March 1957 from where it is operating on Route 35 to Clapham Common, Old Town before its May overhaul. (Alan Mortimer)

The Museum of British Transport opened its doors for the first time on 29th March although at first only smaller items and models were on display. Various larger exhibits were being made ready for display and the chassis of B340 stands amidst the renovation work. The Museum was housed in the former Clapham bus garage for which the land had been originally acquired in 1885 by the London Tramways Company to use as a horse tram depot being taken over by the London County Council in 1899. Becoming eventually a large electric tram depot it survived as such until in late 1950 the first motor buses in the shape of thirty five RTLs moved in. Further rebuilding took place with trams finally departing in 1951. The bus garage closed on 28th November 1958 as part of the cuts imposed that year and two and a half years later reopened as the British Transport Museum. (D.W.K.Jones)

RT2207 is nicely placed to confirm the location of the photograph on Route 152 which in 1961 worked through to Feltham Station. As a matter of interest the original bus to carry this fleet number was one of six fitted with two pedal control and fully automatic gearboxes being garaged then at Turnham Green. The passage of time and three overhauls later now leaves the Merton driver of this RT2207 to contend with the normal RT gearbox and controls.
(Ron Wellings)

RTW265 garaged at Tottenham heads for Victoria down Stoke Newington Road under trolleybus wiring which by the end of the year would be unused. The Savoy Cinema is showing the film 'Fury at Smuggler's Bay' and a doomed trolleybus follows along behind. A Rover P4 car is parked at the kerbside. (A.B.Cross)

West Ham garage trainers RM1 and RM50 take temporary refuge within Stamford Hill depot on 3rd June. The distinctive variation of the front offside wheel arch and the lighter coloured direction indicator on RM1 is evident. Although RM1 is now just seven years old it had been on 31st July 1959 that it last earned any revenue in passenger service and was to perform duties in its newer role as a trainer until withdrawn in 1972. RM50, delivered to Aldenham works in September 1959 from Park Royal first entered passenger service in February 1960 before being demoted temporarily to learner duties. It was to meet a premature end in a garage fire at Walworth in March 1973. (Bespix)

Having reached its last resting place in the yard of W.North of Leeds, AGX526 begins to take on a look of neglect on 11th November. Having first entered service in July 1933 after the formation of the LPTB on 1st July 1933, the chassis with LGOC built body number 13573 was given fleet number STL193 and was one of the first new buses to be put into service under the new legal owner. The STL was withdrawn from service in October 1947 although by then carrying similar body number 13568. The vehicle was converted to a 5 ton tower wagon as shown here and in the 1952 book of this series, becoming 722J in the service fleet. It was used to keep overhead trolleybus wiring in good order until eventually withdrawn in June 1960. The vehicle therefore gave a total of nearly thirty seven years service to London, albeit in two distinctly differing roles. (John Gascoine)

By now eleven months old, Hanwell's RM552 works Route 255 on 5th October which had replaced trolleybus route 655 in November 1960. The route number 255 had lain dormant since its use between 27th May 1936 and 6th October 1937 on a daily route operated by Kingston garage with single deck Q class buses between Feltham and Teddington. (J.H.Aston)

A cold and atmospheric scene shows RT4675 in use on Route 496 having momentarily stopped at St.James' Church, Gravesend. The message on the hoarding might not be strictly true at this juncture given the problems this type of weather usually posed to electric train operation. The bus first entered service in red livery from Upton Park garage in February 1954 carrying body number 8892. On its second overhaul in June 1961 it gained its new green livery, being fitted with body number 8511 which was first mounted on RT4634. (D.Trevor Rowe)

The first numerical sequence of new Green Line RTs ran from RT3224 to RT3259 and all entered service in August 1950 from Romford London Road garage for use on Routes 721, 722 and the seasonal 726. Except for their special livery of Lincoln green with central band of pale green and raised Green Line motif affixed between decks on each side, they were no different to other RTs although they carried body classification RT8/1. Leaving Golders Green station forecourt RT3259, the ultimate in the series, carries very few passengers for its journey on Limited Stop service 726 back from Whipsnade Zoo to Romford via London. (Alan Mortimer)

The chassis of ex-STL1246 was used in this hybrid vehicle which carries a Strachan low height 55 seat body retrieved from another of T.Burrow & Sons Ltd.'s vehicles in May 1956. It is seen at their Wombwell depot and yard which is littered with remains of conversion work on 19th February. Later in its career this combination would be used as a tree lopper attending to low height branches and greenery. When owned by London Transport the bus always carried an LPTB highbridge 56 seat body. (Roger Holmes)

Once RT155 and now the property of Leon Motor Services of Finningley as their fleet number 47, this bus had been disposed of by London Transport to Bird's Commercial Motors in February 1958. It originally entered service in July 1947 when it carried a Park Royal body. Now fitted with a Weymann example of identical appearance originally borne by RT416 it looks very presentable in its new colours with an AEC triangle affixed to the radiator as it stands in Doncaster bus station on 1st July.

Edgware staff frequently left vehicles parked along the access road to the garage and here in early summer sunshine TD114 waits for its next call to duty on Route 240A between Edgware and Mill Hill East Station. The blind for the twenty one minute journey is silent on the route taken despite its radical difference from the 240 between Mill Hill and Mill Hill East. By the close of the year only seventeen of this class, which once totalled 131 vehicles, would be licensed for service, the majority being garaged here at Edgware although Kingston still held a very small number.
(D.W.K.Jones)

Kingsbury Square, Aylesbury could usually be relied on to provide something of transport interest with buses of United Counties, London Transport, Red Rover and City of Oxford turning here for many years. Routes included the 359 to Amersham, for many years a joint UCOC/LT operation. Here RF697 carries the registration of former RF517 which had been one of the original trio to enter service as OMO buses in March 1954. In a rather complicated renumbering exercise carried out on 28th March 1956, the original RF517 was renumbered RF697, with RF697 becoming RF298 and RF298 receiving fleet number RF517. With their newer identities RF697 was eventually scrapped while the other two involved enjoyed more illustrious futures, RF517 being preserved and RF298 exported to Pakistan. (Ron Wellings)

Two RT class vehicles are about to enter the Brighton Road from Crunden Road, the operating crews no doubt having refreshed themselves within the facilities offered in the Croydon garage canteen. RT2107 carries body number 1591 and is garaged at Streatham which was to be its last operating base before withdrawal from passenger service in March 1964. The following bus, RT1227, saw a lengthier period of service not being withdrawn until January 1970. The picture would have been taken on a Saturday which was the only day of the week in 1961 on which the 159 ventured south of Thornton Heath. (Alan Mortimer)

RM615 is viewed in Pancras Road outside Kings Cross Station in March having only entered service the previous month with the introduction of the ninth stage of the trolleybus conversion programme. New route 239 replaced trolleybus 639 between Hampstead Heath and Moorgate, Finsbury Square and was operated from Highgate garage. This RM only remained at HT until July when it was delicensed to reappear in service in November from Wood Green in stage twelve of the conversion scheme. (David Berwick)

In its early years of service the RM class had many shortcomings , one of which was the jerking effect of the automatic gearbox. In an early experiment to overcome this Hanwell garage exchanged most of their month old RMs in December 1960 for new vehicles fitted with semi-automatic control providing manual operation. RM537 entering service in that month was one of these buses. Here it stands at the now obliterated Frays River terminus at Uxbridge as duty number HL23 on Route 207 while advertising BOAC's use of Boeing 707s on its service to the USA and Canada. (R.H.G.Simpson)

Stratford Broadway, long before the vast redevelopment of this busy interchange situated on one of the main routes to the eastern counties, shows two RTs taking a well deserved rest on the cobbles. Nearer the camera RT730 is one of the five of the class provided on Monday to Friday by Barking garage for trolleybus replacement Route 162 which by now ran between here and Mayesbrook Park. The route had reached this previously unserved part of the Becontree Estate via Lodge Avenue in a shake up of services on 11th October. Previously it had run north from Longbridge Road to Little Heath. Behind RT3411 operates out of Upton Park garage and has turned short at the Broadway before returning to Upminster Park Estate. (Ron Wellings)

The carriage stock alongside RT4740 at Tilbury has only another year to go and already the gantries for the electrification of the old London Tilbury and Southend Railway have started to appear in this picture taken on 15th March. The Grays RT on its way to the Ferry is now entering its third year of actual service although it is seven years old and still to receive its first overhaul. It carries Weymann built body number 8981 and was one of a large number of RTs and RTLs placed in store immediately upon delivery and which entered service in the following years. (Roger Partridge)

Elmers End garaged RT279 appears to be reversing out of Croydon garage into a rather deserted Brighton Road. Possibly some obstruction or a surfeit of vehicles prevents access and the driver will instead go round to the back entrance. No doubt the crew will be hoping that the queue of passengers at the bus stop opposite will have been cleared by someone else before they commence their journey in this Park Royal bodied RT back to Oxford Circus. (Alan Mortimer)

Route 215A was a new service which commenced in June 1954 operating on a Monday to Saturday basis between Kingston and Downside effectively replacing the short journeys to Church Cobham on the main 215 which continued on to Ripley. TD type buses were used from its inauguration and TD128 from the second batch carrying Mann Egerton bodywork is viewed at Esher about to continue its journey to Downside. (Alan Mortimer)

RTWs were the type of bus allocated to Route 15 for many years, eventually being replaced in the spring of 1964. Upton Park had RTs in 1961 for their work on routes 40, 86, 101, 145, 147 and 175 but they were not uncommon on the 15 route due to certain cross workings. Here RT879 ventures along the Edgware Road in sunny but cold weather conditions. The lamppost with its ornate base is a reminder of an era when decoration came before costs, an idea foreign in today's quest for economy. (Alan Mortimer)

The chassis of this vehicle first entered service in June 1945 fitted with a Duple body built to utility specification and was numbered D86 by London Transport. It can be seen as such in the 1951 book of this series. Withdrawn by the Executive in April 1953, it was disposed of to W.North & Sons of Leeds. Later in that year it was acquired by T.Burrows & Sons of Wombwell along with two other examples from the Daimler class and all three were rebodied with new Burlingham 61 seat rear entrance bodies with doors in 1957 or 1958. Caught by the camera in Wakefield bus station on 24th May it is in use on the long thirty nine mile route which took five hours to complete. The bus now carries fleet number 82 and displays route details: Wombwell, Barnsley, Wakefield and Leeds. (Roger Holmes)

Saunders bodied RT1832 had originally entered service in July 1950 carrying a Park Royal body. It is seen at the Shoreditch Church terminus of Route 47 during July, the bus being one of a large number of RTs which Catford garage operated for many years. It was in July on the 19th that the 47 route was extended daily to Stoke Newington as part of trolleybus conversion stage 11. The 'home made' bus stand notice fixed to the bottom of the lamppost seems to indicate that problems are beginning to arise from the selfish attitudes of other road users. (David Berwick)

Still carrying the Park Royal body with which it first entered service in June 1943, ex-G66 proudly carries its chassis maker's name at the top of the radiator in this January view. Metal plates show its current fleet number as R0696 and its garage allocation as Perth. The bus appears to be in a remarkably pristine condition for an eighteen year old utility built vehicle. It was to follow the same career as the other W.Alexander and Sons Guy Arab shown within the pages of this book working in Perth, even to its disposal to the dealer, Dunsmore of Larkhall for scrap in 1962. (Ray Stanmore)

Ex-B9 is much altered again when compared with the picture of the bus which appeared in the 1955 book of this series. It now carries a 1949 ECW built body which had originally graced a rebodied 1931 Leyland Titan TD1 chassis registered CK4403. With a much lower mounted PV2 type radiator, its transformation into a post-war looking BTC product is complete for its operation by Crosville Motor Services Ltd. prior to disposal in October 1960. The Atomic Power Constructors (Trawsfynydd) Ltd. acquired several of these ex-London Bristols between 1959 and 1962 from Crosville putting them to work for the transport of construction site employees. Here it stands in the typical grey and wet scenery of Blaenau Ffestiniog. (Alan Mortimer)

RT4634 had latterly been garaged at Cricklewood but now on 2nd April is used by Middle Row necessitating the use of a garage plate to hide its W code. This was a temporary loan to this normally RTL shed as in May the bus entered Aldenham Works for its second overhaul to be outshopped in Country Area livery in line with a number of other members of the class in June. Edgware bus station provides the resting place on Sunday 2nd April for the bus which appears to be confused as to which route it is working. It carries 18B in the main route box together with the via point blind for the 18B which never ventured out on a Sunday and in 1961 did not run further north than Harlesden. The canopy and side blinds correctly show 18. (Roger Partridge)

North End Road, Fulham to this day still attracts the hordes of shoppers presenting similar difficulties as here with people using the road as freely as the pavements. RTL910 in service on Route 91 carries the destination Hounslow West Stn. which after 7th October was the furthest point west reached by Saturday workings, London Airport Central being restricted to Monday to Friday operation. (C.Carter)

With blind reset for the return journey, RLH51 trundles over the railway bridge in St.Albans Road at Watford to turn at Leavesden Road followed by a Lambretta scooter and an RT on Route 318. The bus was to remain in use until disposed of in March 1965 to Office Cleaning Services Ltd. for whom it initially worked in Bristol. A railway enthusiast ignores the bus and concentrates on the activities of the London Midland Region below the bridge which is in the process of being widened. (Alan Mortimer)

The dealer W.North of Leeds not only dealt with the disposal of many of London's time expired bus and coach fleet but also on occasion tackled the service fleet too. Having been disposed of in April 1960, this former breakdown tender number 436W now looks dejected on 21st October with only its registration number providing a clue to its ancestry. The chassis dates from 1931 when it entered service with the East Surrey Traction Company as T258 on Green Line work fitted with a Ransomes 30 seat front entrance coach body. It was withdrawn in 1939 and along with fifteen sisters was converted to a staff ambulance in September 1939 and given its service fleet number. Early in September 1940 the body received minor blast damage and was scrapped in November. A decision was taken to re-use the chassis and in September it reappeared mounted with service body number 9332 still carrying the same fleet number. Basically it was a replacement for 399W which had been destroyed by enemy action at Upton Park around the same time as the ambulance was damaged. It then spent the next eighteen and a half years in its newer role giving a total life span for the chassis of at least thirty years. (John Gascoine)

Standing on the Waterloo stand which is now the Red Arrow garage, RM39, a Poplar garaged bus since January 1960, carries route blinds for the peak hour short journeys on Route 48 as far as St.Pauls. The misleading 5 shown in the offside route number box proves how easy it was to forget the existence of this rather remote indicator. Both routes evolved from Stage 4 of the trolleybus replacement scheme in November 1959 but the 48 was to be withdrawn between Aldgate and Waterloo in trolleybus conversion Stage 12 on 8th November of the year under review and partly replaced by route 4A. (Ron Wellings)

From left to right class K/2 trolleybus 1252, class K/1 1284 and RM637 head rows of similar vehicles parked within Wood Green depot/garage on 6th November. Two days after this picture was taken trolleybus service 641 would be replaced by motorbus service 141 in the 12th stage of the replacement programme while the 269 route had been in existence since 26th April with the 10th stage of the conversion programme. The trolleybuses are all Leyland products with seating for 70, new in March 1939 and eventually disposed of in December of the year under review. The RM first entered service in April from Wood Green. (John Gascoine)

Holloway (J) garage alongside the rear of the properties in Kingsdown Road was eventually closed on 4th September 1971, the site having been associated with passenger transport since the 1870s when used initially in the horse bus era as a depot with stables. This is the view from Holloway Road made possible by some rebuilding work carried out in the 1930s. Awaiting further use on 20th August, RT1666 is a few months away from sale to Bird's Commercial Motors. It now carries Weymann RT3 type body number 1702 in lieu of its original Park Royal RT example numbered 3628. Further members of the class together with one of the private hire RFs allocated to this garage fill the view now completely lost in time. (Roger Partridge)

RT2677 operates a short working on Route 36B to Peckham near its home garage of Rye Lane. Supermarkets had arrived by 1961 although still small by today's standards and the example the bus is passing on the Edgware Road draws your attention to jellies at 7½d, evaporated milk at 1/1d and tomato ketchup for 1/- among other goods. (Alan Mortimer)

In order to free more route numbers for trolleybus replacement motorbus routes, the night group of routes in the two hundred series were renumbered by ingeniously replacing the initial 2 with the letter N on 28th September 1960. Standing on the Holloway (J) garage approach on 20th August, RT4721 still displays blinds used for its night-time activities. Route N92 (previously 292) operated between Trafalgar Square and Highgate, Archway Station having replaced the all night tram service on Route 35 in 1952. (Roger Partridge)

With the completion of the road lowering under the railway bridge at West Drayton a restructuring of the routes in this area took place on 15th March. Double deckers were still unable to use the direct route from Uxbridge via Yiewsley High Road for another year due to the bridge carrying the Western Region line to Vine Street, Uxbridge. The result was that the long standing 222 number disappeared from the area for ten years, the service to Hounslow being transferred to 223 and 224 was strengthened between Uxbridge and West Drayton. This was partly achieved by the introduction of a 224C between those points on Mondays to Fridays with a peak hour extension via Sipson Road into London Airport Central. RF521, formerly RF302, waits at Uxbridge to depart on the peak hour working. Note that, although by this time they had largely fallen out of use, new route number plates for the bracket above the entrance were produced. (Ron Wellings)

One hopes the Bedford lorry driver with his precarious load takes a wide enough berth to clear RT3319 which is going about its business on Route 39 to Parliament Hill Fields. The gentleman on the left of the picture appears to be heading for the public toilets in the middle of Tottenham Court Road outside Warren Street Station where a wash and brush up is offered for 3d by the Metropolitan Borough of St.Pancras. Route 39 had been extended from Camden Town to the terminus the bus hopes to reach unscathed with the 9th stage of the trolleybus conversion programme on 1st February and this RT is one of the Holloway contribution to the route which it shared with Battersea. (David Berwick)

RT1541 stands in the private road alongside Enfield garage displaying the 'lazy blind' used for the sixteen minute long 121 route. Trolleybus wiring is supported by the stanchions for the Hertford Road services using the garage forecourt when working only as far as Ponders End. In December 1963 this bus was returned to service from overhaul in Country Area livery and operated from Hatfield garage. (Ron Wellings)

Former Q69, still basically in original condition, is viewed on 24th September parked in the grounds of St.James' Hospital, Gravesend when owned by the Gravesend Old People's Welfare Committee, as neatly shown in the rear route box. This 4Q4 type Country Area bus first entered service in October 1935 and except for seating alterations which reduced the original capacity from 37 to 35 by the removal of the double seat beside the driver and the provision of a full width cab together with bulkhead incorporating a centre door for driver access in August 1936, the bus remained without further major alteration. These particular pictures illustrate the very short overhang of the Birmingham Railway Carriage and Wagon Company bodywork fitted and now painted in a light green and cream scheme. Although sold for preservation in April 1963 sadly its present condition is unknown. (Roger Partridge)

Disposed of in June 1958, ex-RTL40 with Park Royal body numbered 6683 in the London Transport series brings a London touch to the streets of Perth some 415 miles distant. Seen within the town, intending passengers collect their packages before boarding for the eleven mile journey to Errol beside the Firth of Tay on the service operated by A & C McLennan of Spittalfield. (Alan Mortimer)

Unmistakably an ex-STL although its registration number, CGF772, might confuse since it was one of only three STLs to carry these letters more common on contemporary London trolleybuses. This was once STL1985 of which a nearside picture appears in the 1952 book of this series. Having first entered service in June 1937 and disposed of in March 1951 it managed to escape the attentions of the scrapping process then employed at Daniels of Rainham ending in the condition seen here by 1961. Sadly nothing further is known of its history after this year. A Ford Thames van, a derivative of the very first Escort car and the bonnet of a Fordson Thames lorry complete this picture taken at Wanstead Park. (B.Rackman)

RT991, en-route for London along Chiswick High Road as a relief on Route 704, looks a little dusty. In London Transport ownership from October 1948 through to October 1963, initially it carried body number 2270 but was disposed of to the Cape Electric Tramways with this body, number 1882. Double deck relief vehicles could be seen on the vast majority of the Green Line routes at the time before the decline of this prestige network set in during the early 1970s. The routes which served Windsor always used proportionally more of these vehicles. (R.H.Simpson)

Ex-RT58 unfortunately only saw service with the Ayrshire Bus Owners (A1 Services) consortium of Ardrossan for a period of around twelve months. Repainted into a new colour scheme, a longer period of use may well have been envisaged but it was withdrawn in July 1962 to be returned to Bird's Commercial Motors, the dealer who had originally received the bus from LT in April 1960. It is standing on some rough ground in Ardrossan with blind set for Stevenston (Pillar Box), a destination which suggests a distinct lack of landmarks in that place! (J.C.Walker)

Initially RF289 through to RF513 were delivered to the Executive as Central Area 41 seat buses all classified 2RF2. With the passage of time various members were converted to Green Line coaches, others were renumbered and various seating alterations culminated in a variety of codes being in use at their respective times of withdrawal. RF343 was one of a number converted to OMO at the time of its December 1964 overhaul, re-entering service with seating reduced to 39. Three years prior to its conversion it is seen here operating from Muswell Hill garage and about to depart from Golders Green Station on Route 210. (D.A.Ruddom collection)

On 10th April RTW147 is seen turning out of Bounds Green Road at Wood Green on its way to Tottenham garage upon return from overhaul at Aldenham Works. Trolleybus wiring is still in place for routes 521/621 from North Finchley and, to the right, for 629/641 from Enfield and Winchmore Hill. A Humber saloon followed by a rare commercial version of the Morris Oxford/Cowley Series II introduced in 1954 add to the air of incredibly relaxed driving conditions. (A.J.Douglas)

It is said the Scots have an eye for a bargain and the chassis of the famous first post-war RT402, just eleven years old when acquired with the 1954 body once carried by RT4820, must have been an opportunity not to be missed by H.Brown (Garelochhead Motor Services) in March 1958. Now carrying its new owner's colour scheme complete with local telephone number 200 the bus was given fleet number 23 and waits at Helensburgh on 19th May. The old buildings, weighing machine and announcement boards add to a picture of an age now lost. The board in front of the bus appears to be advertising a Sunday tour while that next to the weighing machine is headed 'Granny Kempock for Gourock' and presumably gives ferry departure times. Kempock Point is on the opposite bank of the Clyde from here next to Gourock. (A.J.Douglas)

Ex-STL2684 makes a fine subject for the camera in January sunshine avoiding the long shadows within the City of Dundee while in use on their route 28. Ten of these Weymann bodied AEC Regent Mark IIs were acquired via Bird's Commercial Motors in 1955 while in the background one of the thirty Craven bodied AEC Regent Mark IIIs, which reached Dundee through the same dealer in 1956, can be seen. Interestingly the London fleet number bonnet plate has been retained while the paint scheme is reminiscent of that worn when it first entered service in the capital, even to the roof colour being projected downwards at the corners. The large M carried beneath the nearside sidelight indicates the vehicle is garaged at Maryfield. (Ray Stanmore)

Chieftain was the fleet name used by J.Laurie & Co. who acquired a sizeable fleet of ex-London RTLs. Number 47 was once RTL1464 which had originally entered service in London during March 1953 and is seen eight years later at Laurie's Burnbank garage. The entire operational fleet of ex-RTLs: 11-15, 30, 38, 39, 41, 51, 52, 336, 357, 1403, 1431 and 1464, were acquired by Central SMT on 1st October of the year under review. Ex-RTL37, which had also been owned, had burnt out sometime earlier and was disposed of before the takeover. (Ron Wellings)

New route 315A was introduced on 7th June of the year under review to operate between Hatfield Station and Hitchin. The long standing 303/303A was diverted through the recently developed part of Welwyn Garden City at Knightsfield and this route maintained a service through the lightly trafficked section at Ayot Green between the Garden City and Old Welwyn. It also replaced the Saturday afternoon journeys to Hitchin on 340B. RT3627 stands at Welwyn Garden City Station with a neat arrangement on the blind to describe this lengthy name without abbreviation. The bus, having been returned to service after receiving an overhaul in October 1960 with body number 1883 first carried by RT634, is garaged at Hatfield. This was to be the last operational base for it as after storage it was exported for further service in Ceylon. (Ron Wellings)

The 177A in 1961 provided the service to the Abbey Wood Estate which is now contiguous with Thamesmead and during the day on Mondays to Fridays the service which otherwise operated from Woolwich was extended to and from New Cross Gate. On 6th December Abbey Wood's RT792 waits to return eastwards at New Cross garage. The blind display however is for the main daily working of the 177A from Woolwich. A fairly new Ford Popular also stands within the garage precincts while one of New Cross's new Routemaster acquisitions for Route 141 can be seen in the background. (John Gascoine)

Now minus its roof box fitting, ex-RT1481 in the ownership of Cunningham's Bus Service of Paisley as their fleet number 18 stands empty except for the driver in the town just prior to its departure for the Renfrew Ferry. This Craven bodied bus, one of a hundred and twenty supplied by the Sheffield manufacturer, now follows even more closely the lines of the previous large order for double deck bodies completed for W.Alexander & Sons Ltd. in 1948 which were mounted on Guy Arab III chassis and given fleet numbers RO583 to RO607. The AEC triangle now carried in place of the London Transport totem at the top of the radiator is a nice touch. (Alan Mortimer)

A question is posed by this photograph of a modified pre-war Leyland STD body mounted on a chassis with an unfamiliar registration. The picture of this fairground vehicle was taken at Garvock in Scotland on 20th August. The upper deck above the bottom of the window line has been professionally removed and the original roof replaced en-bloc complete with the roof route number box. VD4437 is carried by the Leyland TD4 chassis but it is not known if this is the original STD unit or a totally alien example, possibly belonging to the Lanarkshire VD registration. (Terry Blois)

Route 163A was a Sunday only service which, between October 1959 and May 1963, operated from Camberwell Green through to Woodlands Estate at Plumstead. Standing beside the administrative building at Walworth garage, New Cross based RT2077 waits to take up duties to the eastern terminus at Plumstead. (Ron Wellings)

Having reached the end of their working lives, two former Sutton Daimlers, from left to right D276 and D231, stand in the yard of Charles Coppock, a passenger vehicle dealer of Sale, south west of Manchester. Both vehicles had reached this uncompromising yard having been previously operated by the Executors of S.Ledgard and Sons, Leeds and were to make one more journey before the year ended to Shave, a dealer situated in the Manchester Dock complex, who unceremoniously reduced the pair to scrap. (Michael Lockyer)

A very quiet day in February finds RT3583 traversing the empty Bellevue Road with a few passengers sharing its journey to South Wimbledon Station. Having received its second overhaul in January 1960 it now carries body number 7327 which once graced the chassis of RT3490. Merton garage was its operational base from April 1956 through to March 1964 when it was transferred to nearby Sutton garage. It was in July 1969 that Wombwell Diesels Co.Ltd. were to receive this vehicle which had originally entered service in September 1952. (Ray Stanmore)

Eventually withdrawn from service and delicenced in May 1962, this Leyland Tiger PS1 with Mann Egerton bodywork, fleet number TD130, was then unceremoniously moved to other garages for storage until sold in January 1964 to Hills (Patents) Ltd. of Staines. After a period of four years with its new owners it was acquired by the National Trolleybus Association extending its life still further. At Edgware Station on 11th June, looking decidedly past its prime, it attracts a couple of passengers before departing on Route 240A for Mill Hill East Station. (John Gascoine)

R.C.Doughty & Sons of Kings Lynn acquired ex-RTL7 in March 1958 together with two others of the class, none of which were more than ten years old and all having received overhauls at Aldenham only two years earlier - a bargain! In wintry conditions it has proved prudent to provide a radiator cover, though right now it appears more wet than cold. The Park Royal manufactured body is of the RT8/2 variety but little use is made of the generous blind apertures which suggests, together with the background, that maybe the main use is for the transport of workers to one or other of the food processing factories which abound in this region. (Alan Mortimer)

This particular use of the route number 399 was notably short lived. It was a service which started on 13th May 1959 between Aveley (Tunnel Garage) and Bulphan and was withdrawn on 7th June of the year under review being covered by an extension of Routes 328 and 328A from Orsett. Photographed in Grays as it journeys to Bulphan, RT3419 had been returned to service for use at GY after its November 1959 overhaul, previously having been in use in the southern Country Area at Northfleet and Swanley Junction garages. (Ron Wellings)

B.Davenport of Dudley who traded as Blackheath Coaches acquired post war RT403 in June 1958 and then rather surprisingly acquired pre-war RT124 two years later in May 1960. Both buses appear to have had no attention given them since their acquisition, with London Transport transfers still visible on the older vehicle and both still carrying their previous operator's fleet numbers. RT124 although of the batch colloquially known as 'pre-war RTs' actually entered service in April 1941 from Putney Bridge garage with the LPTB built body, number 376, matched to the chassis throughout its LT ownership. RT403 had originally entered service in June 1947 with a roof box Weymann body but received this later design Park Royal body at the time of its last overhaul at Aldenham in January 1958. Viewed in murky conditions in Dudley on an undeveloped piece of land, an atmosphere of gloom pervades this picture. (Alan Mortimer)

Addlestone's contribution to Route 462 which it shared with Leatherhead included RW1, seen at Weybridge Station, a spot familiar to visitors to Cobham Bus Museum annual open days. It is journeying to Leatherhead, having commenced its service at Staines. Indeed the date is Monday 10th April, a week after Easter, and the silver birch with other trees still need to fully reveal their new season's foliage as they often do when the bus enthusiasts descend on this spot. (A.J.Douglas)

RT3602 climbs Holywell Hill, St.Albans while working Route 325 on 7th March. The route blinds used at this time on this service are interesting in that both termini are included on the via blind while the destination box is used to give two via points, in this case Becketts Avenue and Prospect Road to show which way round the Cottonmill Estate, south of the city, the bus would be operating. (Roger Partridge)

Mortlake and Tottenham garages were the traditional providers of buses for Route 73 for many years. In the 1958 rationalisations the route gained an extension beyond Richmond to Hounslow and a small allocation from that garage was introduced which on Sundays worked right through to Stoke Newington. Here, a long way from home, RT369 runs along Church Street, Stoke Newington on 20th August. It is a year before the Beatles might severely affect the trade of the thriving barber shop which announces that it is open all day Thursdays, no doubt to cater for shop workers whose half day this was. The bus carries body number 1965 and was disposed of in February 1964 for further service in Ceylon in company with many sold London vehicles at that time. (John Gascoine)

Hackney's normal allocation on Route 30 in 1961 was RTL but here RT292 has been lent by Loughton garage. It carries a painted H garage plate to cover its L code and is seen at Roehampton waiting to leave for Hackney Wick alongside terraced dwellings called Elizabeth Place dating from 1870. (Alan Mortimer)

West Ham's RM309 is seen in Tramway Avenue just off Stratford Broadway having just passed the erstwhile entrance of the Swan Yard horse tram depot of the North Metropolitan Tramways. The bus is destined for Little Heath, the eastern terminus of Route 162 before it was diverted on 11th October to Mayesbrook Park. This route had been introduced on 3rd February 1960 with the fifth stage of the trolleybus conversion programme.
(Ron Wellings)

On 13th June RTL1603 waits at Stoke Newington Common before departing on a journey to Richmond by way of Route 73 with an Austin A55 Cambridge parked in front. The bus was one of a fairly large number of RT and RTL class vehicles which, although delivered throughout 1954, did not enter service immediately but were put into store, entering passenger service sporadically throughout the next five years. First allocated to Upton Park garage in February 1958 the bus transferred to Tottenham in October of the same year where it stayed until its initial overhaul in October 1961 after which it operated from Hackney. (John Gascoine)

An almost deserted Lea Bridge Road at Leyton is the setting for RT3893 now in Central Area livery having spent its earlier years as a Country Area bus. Rather oddly the Weymann bodied batch RT3857 through to RT3901, delivered in the second half of 1950 in green livery and entering service from WR, SJ, DG, WA, MA, WT and DT garages, were mainly repainted into red livery. This exercise took place during 1959 and eventually was to leave only sixteen of the original forty five buses to carry on performing in the Country Area.
(Ron Wellings)

On 3rd November, just days before first entering service, RML883 makes its way along Ballards Lane at North Finchley on driver familiarisation duties. This rear end view shows the enthusiasm shown by LTE for its new bus fleet with the corner panel sticker. The offside route blind box already displays 104 on which route this new longer variation of the RM family would make its debut in the twelfth stage of the trolleybus replacement programme.
(Bespix)

An interesting February view taken in Stonecutter Street with a Bedford tractor unit and trailer laden with rolls of newsprint for delivery in the days when the Fleet Street area was the working capital of the newspaper industry. The lead vehicle, RM589, is on Route 143 which on 1st February had been rejuvenated from its sleepy suburban years to venture once again into Central London, somewhere it had not gone since the dark days of November 1940. Its extension was in part replacement of trolleybus 517/617, the other route assisting in this task being the 17 on which RM519 behind is working. Both were now the responsibility of the former tram and trolleybus Holloway depot (HT), euphemistically called Highgate to avoid confusion with Holloway (J) garage who formerly worked the 143. (Dave Berwick)

The changed style of frontal appearance on production RMs is clearly shown here at Moorgate. The non-opening upper deck front windows of RM178 awaiting to depart for Chingford Mount on Route 256 compares with the quarter drop windows of RM378 soon to depart for Highgate Village on Route 271. (Lens of Sutton)

A GS class vehicle with seating for 26 passengers carrying an 'Extra' plate beside its CY garage stencil must have made a big impact on a queue of would-be passengers. But GS12 seems to have served in some sort of additional operating capacity while allocated to Crawley garage, perhaps on Route 434 Crawley to Edenbridge whose allocation had increased with the allocation of a GS bus to the route from February 1960. This GS is yet another of the preserved examples today. (D.W.K.Jones)

The various lunchtime works services at Rosherville originated in pre-LPTB days with Maidstone & District and gradually petered out, two surviving into LCBS days. They were timed to take workers home for lunch and bring them back again to the Thameside factories. At the start and end of the day workers were presumably left to trudge up and down to the Overcliffe for transport. The conductor of RT1050 has not bothered to open the roof box and change the route number which should read 488A while the driver of nicely blinded RT1088 makes a quick departure for Alkerden Road at Swanscombe. This was probably in the best interests of his passengers since it was the longest of the services and only gave people at the far end twenty three minutes to swallow their lunch before catching the bus back. Only return tickets were issued and despite the blind displays only bona-fide workers were carried. (Ron Wellings)

In February all Leyland RTW420, one of Battersea garage's complement of these vehicles, operates on Route 31 and is seen here in Kensington Church Street as it continues its journey to the Stanley Arms at Chelsea. This inner west London route can be traced back to September 1911 and still covers much of its original form. The RTW had a much shorter life span, entering service in September 1950 at Putney Bridge and lasting in London Transport ownership until December 1966 when it was disposed of to the Ceylon Transport Board together with the largest shipment of the class made to this operator. (Tom Smith)

Seen in Southend town centre on 18th April, what was once D71 in the London Transport fleet masquerades as Southend Transport number 270 with its newer Massey lowbridge body number 2134. In total thirteen second-hand Daimler CWA6 were purchased by the Corporation in 1954, it having been the intention to acquire eighteen. The resulting five spare Massey bodies were subsequently mounted on new Leyland PD2/20 chassis instead. These buses were the first to be built with three part destination displays adopted as standard after the 1955 co-ordination agreement with Eastern National whose fleet number 1419 (WNO476) disgorges passengers on the far side of the road. (A.J.Douglas)

RF665, a normal resident of Addlestone, carries LH48 duty plates as it waits at Leatherhead railway station before departing on a 462 working to Addlestone. It is now nearing two years since the orange perspex 'Pay As You Enter' signs first appeared but this bus manages to hold on to the discreet example applied by transfer at the top of the nearside windscreen. Converted in May 1958 for one-man operation with a reduction in seating from 41 to 39 the bus would continue in service through to July 1972. (Alan Mortimer)

On Sunday 10th December RM334 together with RM960 stand in the Turnpike Lane bus station. RM334 had previously seen service at Shepherds Bush garage being transferred for use at Walthamstow in November of the year under review. RM960 has completed less than a month's service and is garaged at Wood Green. It shows the new style of upper and lower case lettering first seen at the time of route 141's introduction. The 275 is working a short journey to Woodford Green rather than the full route and borrows a 141 bay in which to lay over although this was the normal Sunday terminus at the western end of this route. (John Gascoine)

RT1869 waits at a rather wet Stonebridge Park trolleybus depot while working on Route 18 in July. Now graced with Weymann body number 1700 which was once carried by RT451 it initially entered service on 1st October 1950 from Wandsworth garage with a Park Royal body and was first used on stage one of the tram conversion programme. Now residing at Alperton garage, its last London allocation, it left the British Isles in February 1964 for Ceylon where it swelled the number of RT family buses with the Ceylon Transport Board. (W.R.Legg)

In the vicinity of the Feathers public house at Merstham, RW2 continues its circuitous route to Woldingham. This nearside view clearly shows the dual door layout of these three Willowbrook bodied buses which were purchased to test the suitability of such vehicles in the Country Area. Entrance transfers adorn the area above the front doorway while the word exit is placed centrally above the second. An orange perspex 'pay as you enter' sign is carried on the front panel while another slip board proclaiming the same message exhorts passengers to have their fares ready and is placed beside the vehicle's duty working plates. (Alan Mortimer)

The Biggin Hill Air Display always draws crowds and before the car became universal many buses and coaches were used for journeys to this event. On 16th June green liveried RT137 from Reigate garage still wears its 'L' plate although one assumes this was not its function on this particular day. It would eventually be disposed of in June 1963 still carrying the body with which it had first entered service in June 1940. Catford garage's RT3374 has been loaned to Dartford for the occasion and stands alongside a Green Line RF. Although the caravan beyond encourages you to enjoy milk, that simmering inside the churns in the June sunshine might not prove too palatable. (John Gascoine)

Standing at the Blackwall Tunnel terminus of Route 56 on 28th January, Athol Street's RTL327 has RM47 of nearby Poplar garage for company operating on the same route. As history shows this was a short term measure with the impending closure of the former garage and transfer of buses and staff with the routes to the former trolleybus depot after which Poplar serviced the route entirely with the RTL class buses. (Roger Partridge)

Former RTL49, which saw service in the capital between January 1949 and February 1958, had already put in three years service with its new owners, A & C McLennan of Spittalfield, Perth when photographed in January of the year under review. Seen in Perth it carries a destination blind for a journey to Stanley situated beside the River Tay just to the north of this once Scottish capital. In the author's view the superb repaint afforded the bus suits this Park Royal built body once carried by RT3040 very well. (Ray Stanmore)

Working as duty MA24, demure GS69 stands at Chesham before its journey on a short working of Route 348 to Bellingdon where the stand was conveniently placed outside The Bull public house. Time is fast running out for this GS as, after its stay at Amersham, it moved to Garston garage in October 1962 where it was only used in passenger service for one month before transfer to Hertford as a trainer for another month. Eventual sale came in May 1963 to Tillingbourne Valley and it met its final fate in September 1965 when it was scrapped following an accident. (Ron Wellings)

RM605 garaged at Highgate operates on Route 276 introduced on 26th April and is seen turning short as it circumnavigates Trafalgar Square before returning to Finsbury Park Station. Fourteen buses were required for this route on Mondays to Fridays while the number dropped to just seven on Saturdays when it only operated until 2.00 p.m. between Tottenham and Trafalgar Square, a terminus which at the time was always referred to as Charing Cross on destination blinds. (Ron Wellings)

Body changes at overhaul meant that some of the earlier 3RT chassis remained in service for longer periods than certain later deliveries. RT310 with its HLX registration is a case in point and it is seen here shortly after its August overhaul when it received this RT8 Park Royal body, number 3656. It would be 1977 before this fleet number, which had graced the streets of London since February 1948, finally succumbed to the Wombwell Diesel Company's breakers' torches. The bus has attracted the photographer's attention not only because of its sparkling appearance but also because an RT working Route 88 at this time was extremely unusual. Riverside and Stockwell provided an all RTL allocation and the SW stencil plate covers a TB code, which garage has generously lent this vehicle. It passes the road reconstruction work taking place at Marble Arch followed by an MG Magnette ZA saloon. (Alan Mortimer)

Seen on a very quiet afternoon in Regent Street, RTL684 makes for Crystal Palace, being a Chalk Farm based bus in use on Route 3 which was shared with Norwood garage. Note the latest amount being paid out for an all correct winning line on Vernons Pools, nowadays a means of a flutter more eclipsed by the National Lottery. (Ron Wellings)

In February RT2107 journeys south to Streatham Common along Bellevue Road on Route 49. This AEC Regent III with its Park Royal body had been allocated to Streatham since May 1959 and remained there until March 1964 being disposed of the following month to Margo's Coaches of London SW16. Why therefore it should still be using a garage stencil plate instead of the by now usual painted code is a mystery. (Ray Stanmore)

Since overhaul in December 1960 RT4338 had been garaged at Hornchurch and in company with another RT awaits departure from Rainham Clock Tower on route 165 for Clockhouse Lane, Hunters Grove. This route number had been introduced on 20th November 1940 when former single deck service 253 operated with T class single deckers was double decked and renumbered, ST type buses taking over the service from Hornchurch garage. (Ron Wellings)

RF5 has now entered its final years of operation with the Executive, the Chalk Farm garage code painted on the side being the last of many locations which have housed this private hire coach. Seen leaving the Wembley sporting complex, which appears to have been well attended, the driver in charge will probably be glad to emerge on to the highway knowing that other vehicles have still to leave the venue. (R.H.G.Simpson)

With wintry conditions in evidence RTW290 stands at the Putney Common terminus. The number of cars clearly demonstrates the increasing competition from privately owned transport. Now garaged at Hackney after its recent overhaul it appears that the fitters are a little over zealous when filling the fuel tank. The 500 strong RTW class remained intact until 1965 when the first sales were made. The long standing, if rather individual, Route 22, operating between Homerton and Putney Common ever since 1916, had been involved with the class since 1951 when they replaced STL class vehicles until they withdrew in favour of RTLs from Battersea in 1965 and Hackney in 1966. (Alan Mortimer)

Emitting considerable visible pollution from its exhaust, RT3509 pulls away from the Rosherville stand on its short 496A works journey in Gravesend to Waterdales. In this picture the lead RT currently carries body number 8122 first carried by RT3650 while RT1050 parked closely behind and ready to take workers to Kings Farm Estate on Route 488A carries roof box type body number 1886, originally mounted on the chassis of RT637. (Ron Wellings)

The transformation of this corner of Park Street, Luton carries on apace with corrugated fencing in place and the new Luton College nearing completion. RF568, with its route blind set for a short journey on the 364A service as far as Breachwood Green, is not venturing the complete length of the route to Hitchin. This RF reached Luton garage in May 1959 having previously seen use at Leatherhead and was to continue to work from its northern area home until its second overhaul in February 1962. (Photobus)

RT4788 waits ready for service on Route 441D at Staines garage which, as this book was being prepared, had been razed to the ground. This view, taken looking into the garage from Greenlands Road, includes the administrative and staff facilities annexe on the right. This particular bus, which was in store at Loughton between delivery in August 1954 and June 1956 when it entered service from Leatherhead garage, received an overhaul in May 1960 emerging from Aldenham carrying body number 1875. Returning to service from Staines garage it was eventually delicensed in October 1963 and disposed of in January 1964, less than eight years revenue service being attained with London Transport. (Ron Wellings)

Negotiating New Cross Gate on its journey to Moorgate, roof box bodied RT2094 makes the right hand turn into New Cross Road, a move impossible in today's one way scheme. This Sidcup garaged bus in the combination now seen with Weymann body number 1795 would be disposed of in 1965 as part of the continuing programme of the withdrawal and sale of chassis carrying this type of bodywork. (Alan Mortimer)

Nicknamed 'Silver Lady', unpainted aluminium panelled RM664 made a great visual impact when it newly arrived at Highgate garage. This was LTE's only attempt at cutting costs on a road vehicle by not painting in the traditional manner. With the Underground rolling stock the situation was accepted and dowdy sets of carriages became the norm. In later years RM664 acquired a similar dowdy appearance and in this picture, although the bus is brand new, variations in the finished panelling caused by the manufacturing process at the rolling mills is clearly evident. Note the use of a garage stencil plate despite the fact that at the time painted on codes were normal practice. This picture is taken at Edmonton Green and the bus is in use on Route 127, its normal occupation while it remained at HT, although it did appear on routes 17 and 276. In December 1962 the bus made the first of its many transfers until it succumbed to normal red paint in July 1965. (Alan Mortimer)

Parked within Peterborough bus station on 20th May ex-RT321 is now in the ownership of J.Morley & Sons Ltd. of Whittlesey. It had been acquired direct from the Executive in February 1959 carrying the Weymann body, number 1695, which had originally graced the chassis of RT446. It was in February 1948 that Park Royal bodied RT321 first entered service from Turnham Green garage and in turn it was to see service from Croydon, Potters Bar and Cricklewood. Only limited use has been made of the various blind box apertures and in this case the destination shows Coates via Whittlesey as its next journey. (J.C.Gillham)

RT2614 en-route for Brockley Rise as duty RL19 on Route 36A is caught in the increasingly heavy traffic being experienced at the start of the 1960s. The driver of the two-colour Vauxhall looks as though he wishes to pull out into the traffic stream but the Rye Lane driver studiously ignores him, being more interested in the photographer. The bus was disposed of by the Executive in April 1963 to Arlington Motors, the dealer with premises in Ponders End and it quickly passed to Lloyd's of Nuneaton in May only to move on to Hartwood Exports of Birdwell in July. It then disappeared into obscurity complete with the Park Royal body number 1613 which it carries here. (Alan Mortimer)

With the rebuilt Hounslow garage as a backdrop, RT913 rests in the sunshine alongside RT933 which is a visitor from Turnham Green garage on 24th June. The Hounslow bus appears ready for a trip to London Airport Central on the 81B route although the via points blind is for the 81A route and the offside route number board shows the parent 81 route. The offside corner advertisement would not be the way you would describe Battersea Fun Fair today, showing the way language usage can change quite quickly. (John Gascoine)

GS15 stands in Hertford Bus Station minus a garage code stencil but having running number 61 and front blind set for a journey on Route 380 to Sawbridgeworth. One GS was allocated to this route which had prior to 7th June been a section of the longer service 388. Oddly this Hertford - Sawbridgeworth section had once before operated separately but then under the 389 number. Brian Speller has for many years kept this preserved GS in superb roadworthy condition and it is a regular attender at many rallies in the southern counties during the summer season. (Ron Wellings)

RT2116 waits at the Northfleet Church terminus of Route 495 on 29th April as duty NF38 before departing to the Christianfields Estate situated in the south east corner of nearby Gravesend. This RT dates from January 1950 being one of an odd batch of six which entered service fitted with a body from the then current float held in the system. It was also the only green liveried one of the batch entering service at Windsor garage. It is now fitted with body number 8090 first carried by RT3618 but continues in green livery. (Roger Partridge)

Ex-RTL550 had been sold carrying body number 4956 in August 1959 to Walsall Corporation Transport and was given their fleet number 201. On 24th May in the year under review it is seen in Cannock employed on Service 17 with rather less route information than provided in its London Transport days. If some people found the overall red with cream band livery used in the capital at the time uninspiring, the Walsall all over blue left even more to be desired. (A.J.Douglas)

Route 134A was a Sunday variant which commenced operation in November 1958 and was to last through until August 1969. It deviated from the main route at Barnet to run to Chesterfield Road and detoured via New Barnet Station and Longmore Avenue. RT3780 garaged at Muswell Hill is in Junction Road at the Archway while two trendily dressed youths of the time eye the photographer. (Ron Wellings)

The interesting history of D167 began with its entry into service as a 56 seat Duple bodied Green Line bus in March 1946. The Daimler chassis was of the CW variety first introduced in 1943, being a development of the pre-war COG5 with first examples being fitted with five cylinder oil engines. As with most London Transport D class it was fitted from new with an AEC 7.7 litre engine. After five years operation from Romford, London Road it was transferred to Merton and repainted into Central Area livery in July 1951 before being withdrawn from service in February 1953. It then passed through the hands of W.North the Leeds dealer, the White Bus Company of Bridlington and the East Yorkshire Motor Service Ltd. before ending up with E.G.Palmer (Fordham & District). This photograph was taken on 3rd June at Fordham, Cambridgeshire and shows the bus in its final condition, still resembling its original appearance. A metal bar across the route box being the only visible alteration that has taken place. (G.R.Mills)

RT4632 makes a manoeuvre not now possible with the pedestrianisation of much of Kingston and the ring road system which has been introduced. It is about to cross the junction with London Road and Fairfield West in the opposite direction to that permitted at the time this book was being written. Having just commenced its journey it is working to West Molesey rather than over the full route to Walton-on-Thames. The abandonment of trolleybuses in this enclave of south west London would not take place until the following year and the wiring in place is for Routes 602 and 603. (Ron Wellings)

RT721 now carries this Park Royal body, number 1990, originally mounted on the chassis of RT711 and would continue to do so until disposed of in September 1964 when it was exported to Ceylon. Well before its departure it is seen operating from Peckham garage heading south down Edgware Road on Route 36 to Hither Green Station. A further reminder of times gone by is afforded by the Black & White Milk Bar, an early example of a fast food chain common in London for many years, its speed of service enhanced by the wide open entrance. (Alan Mortimer)

Negotiating the roads in Grays town centre, RT4794 once carried body number 9227, the highest numbered of the RT class. 9228 was the number given to the LTE/Park Royal body of RM1. On 26th March and now with body number 6996 which it had gained on its July 1959 overhaul it operates on Route 371A to Purfleet Station. It was to be garaged at Grays from the overhaul mentioned above until its next visit to Aldenham Works which took place in June 1963. (Roger Partridge)

The prolific array of direction signs on the lighting standard just being passed by RT1094 confirms this photograph as having been taken at Croydon. Martins Bank Ltd., later absorbed by Barclays, occupies the corner building while the bus in a convoy of traffic makes its way to Farleigh on Route 403B. It had re-entered service at Chelsham garage from its May overhaul carrying this RT3/1 body built by Weymann in the 1948/49 era and from the same batch as that originally carried.
(Roger Partridge)

Twickenham garaged RT297 received its last overhaul in March 1959 re-entering service with body number 1764, ex-RT515. The 'garage under the evergreen oak' as the London Transport Magazine described the small Twickenham building, was the initial home for this RT in its final guise. It was to be based in this south west district of the capital being transferred to Hounslow and later Kingston before finally being delicensed and stored at Fulwell to await disposal in May 1964. As it journeys on Route 90B to Kew Gardens Station it epitomises the quality in which the overall fleet could be found operating during this era of London Transport. (Alan Mortimer)

Having stood unwanted in the Edgware garage yard since being delicensed in December 1960, this Mann Egerton bodied Leyland Tiger PS1, fleet number TD86, was eventually disposed of in February 1962. Since Edgware continued to operate TDs until October 1962 it may be that this one was held on to as insurance for spare parts. Although the photograph was taken on 11th June, gloom seems to sum up the situation for this twelve year old originally purchased as part of a 100 strong batch of single deckers to bridge the gap between the earlier pre-war types which were fast becoming time expired and the RF class yet to appear.
(John Gascoine)

Lightly loaded RT4384 is about to pass over the rubber faced traffic light actuator pad clearly visible in the road surface. In this electronic age such devices have become things of the past. Route 81 has a long history stretching back to 1912 when it first operated between Hounslow (The Bell) and Windsor Castle. Nowadays it still follows much the same course operated by Westlink between Hounslow garage and Slough.

Ex-STL2697 stands outside the 1923 built Widnes garage in Moor Lane on 27th August. The bus was one of four 18STL20s acquired by Widnes Corporation via North, the Leeds dealer, in August 1955. It wears a bright red livery with cream relief as do the other buses in view which include one of the two Leyland bodied PSU1/13s purchased in 1952 and FTF206, a Daimler CWA6 with Duple lowbridge bodywork, one of three purchased in 1945. (J.G.E.Nye)

Hyde Park Corner, Park Lane and Marble Arch were all subject to extensive road works at this time and here RTL1626 heads out of the former east side of the Hyde Park ring road, now the northbound traffic lane of Park Lane, to circumnavigate the extended roundabout at Marble Arch where Tyburn Way is under construction. A crowd of people head towards the rantings on Speakers' Corner while the ladies in the front seat upstairs look with anticipation towards the shops of Oxford Street. This Tottenham based RTL was to receive an overhaul in April of the following year when it would move on to West Ham. (Ron Wellings)

Norwood's RT775 emerges from Crunden Road, South Croydon at the start of its journey to Waterloo on Route 68. This RT now carries body number 1824 first carried by RT575 and it is ironic that with the body interchange system operated by London Transport, RT775 would be disposed of in May 1965 while the lower numbered RT carried on until June 1972 mainly because by then it carried an RT8 type body. (Alan Mortimer)

The business of T.Beckett of Bucknall, Staffordshire was founded in 1930 and they first acquired ex-London buses in the shape of two STLs in 1953 although only as a means of providing spares for other AECs in the fleet. They turned their attentions to the RT in 1956 when they purchased no fewer than nine of the Craven bodied London rejects. In this picture RT1449 leads RT1458 typifying the mainstay of the double deck fleet in 1961, with a line of cars opposite including an Austin Cambridge A55, a Ford Prefect and a Morris Minor. In March 1963 the business was purchased by the Potteries Motor Traction Co.Ltd. but the RTs acquired were never given fleet numbers or operated in service. (A.B.Cross)

On Monday 6th November Trolleybus 1496 and RM428 stand together at the North Finchley terminus alongside the now removed Gaumont cinema. The trolleybus of class L/3 is a Metro-Cammell chassisless vehicle using AEC running units and Metrovick motors and controllers. It stands parked with its booms stowed out of use in the spot where redundant vehicles were often left by Finchley Depot drivers. This view was taken just two days before Route 621 between North Finchley and the Holborn Circus loop was converted to bus operation as Route 221. The RM is in use on Route 17 introduced with the 9th stage of the conversion programme on 1st February and is due to journey the full length of the Monday to Friday service through to Camberwell Green, providing a cross-river connection beyond the capability of the old wire bound routes. (John Gascoine)

Dundee Corporation Transport acquired thirty Craven bodied RTs in 1956 to replace the remaining trams which ran for the last time on 20th October 1956. They were given fleet numbers 211 - 240 and remained in service intact until 1968 when the first were disposed of to be followed by the remainder the following year. Fleet number 237, once RT1515, traverses the city centre wearing its new owner's colours of green and white while in use on Route 36 to Windsor Street. (Ron Wellings)

When first introduced on 1st February of the year under review Route 253 had a Monday to Friday allocation of 52 RMs to carry out the duties on the horseshoe shaped route. Operating between Aldgate and Tottenham Court Road, Howland Street over roads previously served by tram 53 and trolleybus 653, the route requirements until conversion to motorbus had always been supplied by Holloway Depot. After conversion responsibility was shared initially with Edmonton and then from October with Stamford Hill and gradually this garage assumed the lion's share until its closure. Now the entire complement of buses comes from Clapton. RM406, one of HT's vehicles, journeys down Hampstead Road past the 'Black Cat' Carrera's building while a clippie complete with her Gibson ticket machine walks along presumably to return to her bus which had turned short at Mornington Crescent Station. An RT in use on Route 39 is just about discernible in the far distance by that station. (Ron Wellings)

Returned to service at Shepherds Bush garage after its June overhaul at Aldenham, RTL1498 is arriving in Wells Road at the end of its journey from Hayes on Route 105 with Goldhawk Road station on the Hammersmith and City Line behind. 'The eyes have it' posters which adorned the front of many buses at this time were an enigmatic way of promoting London Transport's advertising facilities. (John Gascoine)

Alperton's RT3056 is seen resting on the large expanse of uncluttered hard standing at the rear of Edgware Station now occupied by the more organised bus station before it departs on a journey to the Empire Pool at Wembley. This was the limit of weekday operations on Route 18 during the year under review although on Sundays it ran through to London Bridge. This was to change in the following January when the route became involved in Stage 13 of the trolleybus conversion. (Ron Wellings)

RF650 first entered service in September 1953 from Two Waters garage as a 41 seat bus carrying the code 2RF2/2. In February 1958 it was re-seated to accommodate 39 passengers being converted at the same time to one-person operation and recoded 2RF5/1. Seen here with the contemporary orange perspex 'Pay As You Enter' sign on the front of the vehicle, enhanced by a slipboard encouraging you to get your 'Fares Ready Please', it stands in the King Street bus station at East Grinstead while working Route 428. (Roy Marshall)

RM528 reached Hanwell garage in December 1960 being one of a fairly substantial number of new vehicles equipped experimentally with manually operated gearboxes to enter service during the month from this garage replacing earlier examples fitted with the normal fully automatic type of equipment. On a quiet Sunday morning it runs down a deserted Ruislip High Street, the only pedestrians being a couple window shopping at Crown Wallpapers. No doubt she intends to set him some DIY project! (Ron Wellings)

This is the low bridge in Headstone Drive which over the years has claimed several normal height double deckers. Although the sign on the left states there is clearance for vehicles up to the height of 13'9" it is not very prominent and in 1961 there was no warning on the bridge itself. RLH60 squeezes under the bridge on Route 230. This was an original Harrow Weald vehicle but in between its first and second overhauls it worked at Hornchurch before returning to HD in December 1960. After disposal in 1969 it was to find its way to Long Beach, California. The fine body lines of a Jaguar Mark I contrast sharply with the functional lines of the bus. (Alan Mortimer)

Three of the new class of RML parked inside Finchley garage awaiting their entry into service have received mischievous attention from someone who has set their front route blinds for three different routes. In the event it was on Route 104 that these new 30' long buses entered service with the agreement of the Transport and General Workers' Union. It was felt at the time that using a larger seating capacity bus, in this case with 72 seats, to replace a 70 seat trolleybus was more acceptable to the Union than using them to replace 56 seat RT family vehicles. In front of RML883, 880 and 882 a trolleybus turntable can be seen let into the floor. (Alan Mortimer)

The Tottenham Court Road one-way system came into operation on 1st May and Palmers Green's RT576 crosses Euston Road on the newly southbound only Gower Street at the point where the east-west underpass now starts its descent. At the time Palmers Green garage's involvement with the route was only at weekends. (Alan Mortimer)

Ex-RTL44 is seen at Kilmarnock about to depart for Ardrossan via Beggs Terrace which is obviously of great significance since it is carried on the destination blind, a slipboard beneath the canopy and on another beside the rear platform in the extreme lower deck window. The operator is part of the Ayrshire Bus Owners' Association. In very non-London fashion the front blind has been converted to outside operation as seen by the repositioned winding handle. (J.C.Walker)

The former Edmonton trolleybus depot received an initial allocation of seventy three RM buses for its involvement in the tenth stage of the conversion programme which took place on 26th April. Trolleybus service 679 was replaced by bus route 279 which operated between Smithfield and Waltham Cross daily and ventured beyond the wires to Flamstead End on Saturdays. This northern section operated from Tottenham Garage on Saturdays and Tottenham Hale on Mondays to Fridays, the bifurcation resulting in route number 279A. RM802 stands by Tottenham Green and was one of the second batch of the type supplied to Edmonton when its remaining trolleybus route, 649, was converted on 19th July. The bus was transferred to Stamford Hill garage in October with the reduction of buses required at EM which occurred that month. (Alan Mortimer)

Within the Belvedere depot of Salisbury United on 15th February what was once G192 and latterly Trans-Rhodes Services of Salisbury, Southern Rhodesia, fleet number 56 survives in use as an office. It had been in operation in London from July 1945 until April 1951 during which time it was exclusively operated by Barking garage. W.North and Sons of Leeds acquired the bus in January 1952 before despatching it to Africa. Some of its original red paintwork shows through the green and cream livery of Salisbury United. This was the last survivor in double deck form of the batch of ex-London Guy Arabs which were mostly rebodied with new Blanckenburg single-deck bodies later in their careers. Note the rear wheel arch which has been faired in and the additional corrugated sheet roof added to lessen the effects of direct heat from the sun on the Massey body. Also visible for good measure is a Bedford CA van, a delectable Austin A35 pick-up and a Morris Minor, all British built. (L.G.Hooley)

CRL4 wears the new experimental light green livery applied during August 1960 at the same time as sixteen Green Line RF coaches were similarly treated. It exits Golders Green station forecourt to continue its journey to Woking on Route 716A and carries an Addlestone garage plate. Officially allocated to Stevenage, coaches often ended the day at the 'wrong' end of the route hence the WY plate. Note the use of the rear offside route number box. A partly obscured pre-war Rover car together with a fine looking air cooled rear mounted engine VW Microbus with reversed registration completes the picture. Note also the additional 'This is London Transport's new Routemaster double-deck Green Line coach' sticker above the lower saloon windows. (Alan Mortimer)

Green liveried RTL1311 passes the 'One Bell' public house in Old Hatfield on its journey to Hitchin on Route 303A. The 303/303A group of routes had long been associated with the Great North Road from Barnet to Hitchin but new towns like Hatfield and Stevenage, development at Welwyn Garden City and other service adjustments resulted in a more and more convoluted journey over the years. This part of Hatfield for example, once the terminus of LGOC summer Sunday routes, is now a quiet cul-de-sac. (Ron Lunn)

The date is 7th February and Crawley garaged RT2520 works a duty on Route 405A between Horsham town centre and Roffey Corner which lies less than two miles away astride the A264 on the main road link with Crawley. As described on the destination blind the 405A worked via Littlehaven as against the main 405 which worked direct between Horsham and Roffey Corner. Some 405A buses did continue beyond Roffey Corner to Crawley and Redhill. (A.B.Cross)

RT3601 waits at Hatfield Station on 2nd March before departure on a Hatfield New Town journey on Route 340B to South Hatfield, Southdown Road. The old Great Northern Railway station buildings form the background, all of which have now been removed in favour of a featureless modern booking hall. The advertising on the hoarding is interesting - one could get hot water installed by Eastern Electricity from £10.16.0 or £2.0.0 off any new gas cooker until 1st April. (Roger Partridge)

In this autumn view RT3189 waits on the traditional 455 stand in Uxbridge bus station before departure on its return journey to High Wycombe, Guildhall as duty HE18. Originally having entered service at Amersham in 1950 as one of the first post-war RTs with full blinds it now resides at its second garage, still maintaining its Buckinghamshire connections. (Ron Wellings)

During its initial stay at Highgate garage the unpainted RM664 could also be seen in use on Route 276 which had commenced service on 26th April with stage ten of the trolleybus replacement programme. This route basically boosted existing bus routes over its entire length and had a short existence being withdrawn after service on 13th August 1963. The RM in its unpainted condition lasted a further two years. This photograph of the bus en-route for Streatham, Telford Avenue was taken on 17th July amid the familiar architecture of Whitehall with the dome of the National Gallery in the far distance. (Bespix)

RT107 passes the familiar outline of the buildings and fencing of Chiswick Works. Having first entered service in May 1940 from Putney Bridge garage, its previous few years have seen it in use as a staff bus being followed with a later period as a learner vehicle. Finally being delicensed in February 1963 it was sold to G.Cohen in September of the same year presumably for scrap. Note the two young bus spotters, one with notebook in hand, on the extreme left of the picture by the Chiswick gates. (R.H.G.Simpson)

There is no doubt as to who can legally use this layby at Haven Green, Ealing Broadway. RT285 uses the stand on Route 83 while it waits to depart as ON6 for Golders Green Station. Between 1960 and 1964 the route had a summer Sunday extension to London Airport and while the blind contrives to show only the weekday portion of the route it is set halfway between the proper weekday display and the Sunday one. (Alan Mortimer)

RT3355 makes its way down a relatively deserted Regent Street en-route to Crystal Palace, being one of Norwood garage's complement for the route it shared with Chalk Farm. The route's long history line can be traced back to the early years of the century in the developmental period of the motorbus. It first reached Crystal Palace in 1913 and enjoyed a forty one and a half year spell from 1939 on running unchanged between Camden Town and Crystal Palace. (Ron Wellings)

The Edgware Road in the vicinity of Praed Street sees RT3942 making its way to Victoria on Route 16. The Mac Fisheries shop which sold fresh fish attracts some window shoppers and it is notable that it has a window. A few years earlier the fish slabs in these shops were usually open to the elements with a distinct smell all of their own. At least now the bread and cakes offered for sale next door by Rosin are not in danger of being tainted by the proximity. The front advertisements on the bus brings home the longevity of a certain soap opera. (Alan Mortimer)

RTL1021 operating from West Green garage runs along Westbury Avenue en-route for Alexandra Park, Victoria Hotel. Apart from turning at Carterhatch rather than Forty Hill and not serving the section beyond Turnpike Lane to Alexandra Park the route remains much unchanged today. It is doubtful however if anyone in 1961, when the route belonged to Enfield and West Green, would have believed you if you prophesied that in twenty nine years time it would be worked by Potters Bar. (Alan Mortimer)

Not a great deal of activity is taking place at Hounslow bus station in this December view with a blizzard in full swing. Only the two buses to the left of the picture can be positively identified of which RT3480 will soon depart on Route 116 with only the route number visible. RF448 accumulates snow but its intention to get to Chertsey on Route 237 is still clear. Boarding points are still clearly in evidence for six of the numerous routes which terminated at this rather unfriendly bus station. (Alan Mortimer)

Edgware's RT1222 turns into the north end of Watford High Street having just commenced its journey on Route 142 to Kilburn Park Station. It will now traverse the complete length of the High Street, a feat impossible today with the partial pedestrianisation of the once main thoroughfare through this busy shopping town. The latest Marlon Brando/Karl Malden movie 'One Eyed Jacks' is showing at the Plaza, Leicester Square.

Chelsham had been the second garage to put the GS class of vehicle into service; Routes 464, 465 and 485 being the lucky recipients in October 1953. Exactly nine years after their introduction they were to be replaced in October 1962 by one man operated RF class vehicles. A year earlier on 21st October GS81 is seen passing through Oxted on its journey to Holland by way of Route 465. Locals had become used to the familiar sight and sound of these little Guy/ECW combinations by the time this picture was taken and some sign of wear and tear is evident on the roof and nearside wing of this example. (John H.Meredith)

In October New Cross based RT209 is viewed complete with crew relaxing between its journeys on Route 21 at Finsbury Square, Moorgate. Originally delivered with a Park Royal body and entering service during November 1947 from Potters Bar, the bus now carries a Saunders built example. Although numerically the fifty eighth post war RT, it would continue in service for many more years to come, eventually being disposed of for scrap to Wombwell Diesels in April 1973. The Vauxhall Victor Series II parked behind has somewhat impeded the RT's approach to the stand. (Tom Smith)

A line up of RTs at the Royal Mews shows the popularity of Windsor Castle for a day trip by public transport in 1961. The red liveried examples to the right are in use on the Saturday and Sunday only extension of Route 81 from Hounslow while RT3629 with a further stable mate carry white on blue route blinds for the special express service on 457 to and from Uxbridge Station. (Ron Wellings)

RT4642 one of Merton's large fleet of RTs works duty AL7 on Route 152 with Feltham Station as its eventual destination. This RT, like others shown in this volume, was due to change its colour scheme, being returned to service from its June overhaul with body number 8880 originally carried by RT4656 and re-entering service in the Country Area from Staines. (Alan Mortimer)

On 21st June new route 261 commenced operation between Arnos Grove Station and New Barnet Station making use of two RTs garaged at Palmers Green. This was the first route to serve Waterfall Road and Church Hill Road and proved a great success. After several changes it is extant today in the much lengthier Route 184 between Turnpike Lane Station and Chesterfield Road at Barnet. At New Barnet Station the route on this day was in the hands of RT590 above and RT768 below, identified by running numbers AD1 and AD2 respectively. The bus with three piece route blind box currently fitted with body number 6179 had a longer period of operation in London lasting until June 1977 whereas the roof box example moved on to pastures new with the Ceylon Transport Board in November 1964 with the body it carries here, numbered 1720. (Ron Wellings)

Bradford City Transport acquired twenty five ex London Transport RTs in 1958 giving them fleet numbers 401 through to 425. Originally they were repainted in the new operator's blue livery with only a single narrow primrose band between decks, the object being to get them into service with the minimum of delay. By 1961 ex-RT177 now wears the standard colour scheme complete with lining out and looks immaculate with rebuilt blind apertures. A trafficator is now fitted beside the driver's cab door while the rear wheel trim is of a much more decorative design than the plain variety worn in London service. In the background trolleybuses can be seen jostling for road space on the system which was eventually to close down on 24th March 1972 outlasting the bus which was disposed of in 1969. (Alan Mortimer)

The East Croydon Station building provides the background to RT947 en-route for Croydon Airport by way of Route 194. Elmers End garage were the custodians of this bus with body number 7767 from its re-entry into service after its May 1960 overhaul until its next which took place in May 1964. The compulsory bus stop is served by buses on routes 12, 54, 119, 130, 130A, 194 and 194A, four of which routes still pass this point today. (Ron Wellings)

Passing through New Cross Gate as it journeys to far off Tottenham, Bruce Grove, RT3300, now graced by the body once carried by RT705, shares the road space with an array of other road users. In later years this bus was exported to Ceylon along with many other such vehicles. Here it represents Holloway garage's small contribution to the route which replaced the north London tram contribution to the former Kingsway Subway tram routes. After nearly nine and a half years the allocation on the 171 was transferred on 8th November of the year under review to the much more logical West Green and Tottenham garages. (Alan Mortimer)

This scene on the Southend Road at South Woodford is now submerged beneath the flyovers and slip roads of the M11/A406 junction but in quieter times Walthamstow's RM182 heads for Manor House on Route 123 which in the previous year had been an extended replacement for the 623 trolleybus. The fitting of various alternative electrical equipment was conveyed by this bus being coded as a 5/5RM5/5, the initial production vehicles having carried the simple 5RM5 identification. A Morris Minor Traveller with its familiar woodwork passes in the opposite direction while an ordinary Morris Minor saloon attempts to overtake the bus. (Alan Mortimer)

A very unusual operation finds Hounslow's red RF363 in use on Green Line route 701. It stands in London Road at Hounslow minus the driver and other photographic evidence suggests he may have gone to see if he can have his real bus back, which presumably had failed on its outward journey to Ascot. What is impressive is the proper blind which has been put into the box rather than the cornflake packet which might be expected today. Equally notable is the large load carried.
(Alan Mortimer)

From 26th April, when Highgate became completely motorbus, their small Sunday allocation on trolleybus route 609 had to be worked with RMs. This lasted until the Finchley operated 609 between Barnet and Moorgate became bus 104 on 8th November. Highgate garaged RM582 journeys to North Finchley at the Nags Head, Holloway on 16th July. Trolleybus wiring is still in place for the Finchley routes 521, 609 and 621, now the only electrically operated routes remaining at this point. (Bespix)

Shepherds Bush based RM324 waits on the Letchford Gardens stand at Harlesden, College Park before leaving on the long run through to West Croydon on Route 220. Three trolleybuses in the background have turned short on Route 662 suggesting that they may be extra duties catering for expected additional traffic for an event at Wembley Stadium. (L.T.P.S.)

Nearing the end of its passenger use with London Transport RT1280 with body number 1561 which it had received in 1957 upon its last overhaul, is now looking a little dowdy. Disposed of to F.Ridler of Twickenham in June 1963 it was eventually exported, made the short sea crossing to the continent and was being used for promotional work in Paris when seen there in 1968. (Alan Mortimer)

Route 233, which had been double decked throughout in March 1959 having operated partly converted for three and a half years prior to this, lives on today in the identical form of Route W3. In 1961 it utilised RTL type vehicles from West Green although at the turn of the year that garage would close and the route would move into the rather more convenient former Wood Green trolleybus depot. RTL835 passes through the Alexander Palace grounds as it journeys on to Finsbury Park Station as duty WG14 on 18th June, the top deck passengers enjoying for a moment the wonderful views across London on this clear summer day. The bus was one of those transferred to West Ham garage in January 1962 on the closure of West Green. (John Gascoine)

RF80 heads north through Watford on its journey to Aylesbury on Green Line Route 707. The coach had been based at Tring garage since receiving its second overhaul in May 1959 and by now must be well used to the long journey from Oxted south of the North Downs through London and over the Chilterns to the Vale of Aylesbury.

Greenhill Motors has a fine array of motor cycles offered for sale in its New Barnet showrooms as CRL4 with its electrically operated jack-knife platform doors open waits for the conductor's bell before continuing its journey to Stevenage on Route 716A. In August the coach would be reclassified RMC4 bringing it in line with the production batch of Routemaster coaches to be received the following year. Trolleybus wiring for Routes 609 and 645 adorns the roadway but by 3rd January 1962 electric traction along this road will be just a memory. (D.W.K.Jones)

Both the ex-London STD class vehicle and the ex-Wallasey Corporation Leyland PD1 with MCCW body parked at Sarajevo on 25th August have had their platforms repositioned for driving on the right hand side of the road in Yugoslavia. For added interest a complete London Transport bus stop and flag have been provided. The registration plate of this STD reads *6X.2001, the star nearly always carried at the time with 6X identifying the area or city in which the vehicle is licensed. (D.Trevor Rowe)

307B was a Saturday only service which ran between the bus station at Hemel Hempstead and Chaulden. It had started in May 1957 and finally ran on 18th October of the year under review, being replaced by additional buses on Route 320. Before its demise RT3028 collects some passengers one Saturday in the bus station which to this day is little more than a large layby. Independent operators survived in this area for many years, two of which can be seen in the background. The leading vehicle is on the Rover Bus Service to Chesham via Bovingdon. (Ron Wellings)

The last of the single deck T class of vehicles were sold in 1963 being Ts785, 787, 790 and 792. This photograph taken inside Garston garage shows T792 now gathering dust, having last seen passenger use in December 1960 when it operated from Tring garage. Unlicenced and parked in the tranquillity of its last resting place, it would never again turn a wheel until February 1963 when it was disposed of to L.W.Vass of Ampthill, Bedfordshire along with two of the others mentioned above. T787 left later for W.North of Sherburn in Elmet, Leeds. RT4563 together with a 2RT2, both unlicenced at the time, can be identified in the line up. (John Gascoine)

Parked at the Finsbury Square, Moorgate terminus two of the newer mode of passenger vehicles which have replaced the trolleybuses now rest before their respective departures to the northern suburbs. RM618 is involved as HT53 on 239 the more recent of the two trolleybus replacement routes represented having been introduced on 1st February replacing 639. The RM further from the camera waits to depart for Highgate Village on Route 271 which replaced 611 in 1960. Of interest are the white painted rings on the street lamp. Could they date from the war? The advertisement on RM618 indicates that British Railways were still actively seeking freight traffic in 1961.

Hendon's RT194 waits at the London Bridge terminus of Route 13 before commencing its journey to Golders Green Station. While the driver has his sleeves rolled up, the conductor has perched himself up on the bonnet which by now must be a little warm. One can almost savour the odour permeating from the well stocked window display of the branch of Mac Fisheries across the road. The bus served Londoners from October 1947 until it left for pastures new in June 1963, being last heard of in use on promotional work on the streets of Paris. (Alan Mortimer)

RLH44 makes an interesting comparison with the picture which appeared in the 1952 book of this series taken when the bus was almost new. Now garaged at Amersham, the most obvious addition is the direction indicators now protruding like ears from the relief colour between decks. The number plate has been repositioned within the stone guard shell of the radiator, it previously having been mounted beneath. The wheel trim or 'dustbin lid' which now adorns the rear wheel is a nice touch although the side advertising rather detracts from the gleaming uncluttered earlier view of the bus. Here the bus heads up Watford High Street en-route to Chesham on Route 336 the Sunday operation of which was withdrawn between Latimer Lane and Watford after 25th October. (Photobus)

RT1728 was overhauled in August 1961 and allocated to Peckham garage but it is evident from this picture taken on 13th August that it was initially borrowed by Tottenham garage. This was an all Leyland shed at the time, apart from the small batch of RF class buses for Route 236 and so this was a very unusual occurrence. (W.R.Legg)

Highgate's RM740 waits at the Holborn Circus terminus in Charterhouse Street. Like its trolleybus predecessor 659, route 259 worked clockwise only round the Holborn loop - there never having been an anti-clockwise 559. The bus stop flag carries a notice announcing that 'starting July 19, bus 243 will stop on the other side of the road'. This was the Monday to Saturday replacement for trolleybus service 543 which did have a 643 partner which was not replaced. The three month old RM has obviously required attention to its front registration plate and the '0' has been replaced with the squared off variety used on trolleybuses. (Michael Rooum)

Smith's Coaches of Reading were the proud owners of ex-RT54 from May 1956 having acquired it via the well known dealer, W.North, to whom it had been sold by London Transport in December 1955. It was during that year that the first mass disposals of this type, collectively known as the 'pre-war RT class' took place. It is seen here beneath the wiring of the Reading trolleybus system. The bus served ten years with Smiths and was purchased for preservation in 1967 subsequently having a plethora of owners.

The complete operational history of this Park Royal bodied Guy Arab II spanned the years 1945 through to 1965. Delivered to London Transport as G324 it was put to work in December 1945 from Upton Park garage joining many of its contemporaries and spending its entire London period at this East End building. Withdrawn in December 1952 it then passed to W.North & Sons in February 1953 being purchased by Burton Corporation and reconditioned by Roe prior to entry into service. It is seen on 25th March working a service to Beam Hill carrying the maroon with centre band of cream relief livery then current. Withdrawn in December 1964 it was despatched to Evan, a dealer of Warsborough Dale, Barnsley in January 1965 for scrap. (R.Marshall)

In 1961 the night bus network was a very small affair compared to today and there were only seventeen such specified routes. In the early morning gloom of a recent shower RTL1115, having completed its night shift on route N91 between Liverpool Street and Willesden garage, waits for its daytime task to be allocated at this all Leyland garage. The RTL class began to see the depletion of their number from 1958 culminating with the last being used in service during 1968. This particular bus was disposed of in May 1964 with its current body, num-ber 5710, to a most unusual business, the King Korn Stamp Company of London N12. (Ron Wellings)

H & C Transport Ltd. of Garston acquired RT221 from Bird's of Stratford upon Avon in March 1959. In the following month they also received RT205 which obviously needs further attention to bring its appearance up to the standard now enjoyed by RT221. Both commenced service in 1947 at Potters Bar and both were to be withdrawn in 1968, initially being disposed of to F.Cowley the Dunchurch dealer. Having had its front roof box removed the nicely presented RT presents a mirror image of the one still needing attention. (John Gascoine)

As elsewhere in this book and others in the series, buses in Station Road, Finsbury Park had a background which appeared to be caught in a time warp. New Cross garaged RT3714 is waiting to depart on Route 179 to Grove Park. This route number was brought back into use on 6th January 1952 with the 6th stage of the post-war tram conversion programme and subsequently in 1958 was extended north from Farringdon Street to this point. However on 8th November of the year under review it was withdrawn being replaced here by a new version of 4A and a new 141A and on the former tram section by new 141. An unusual case of a trolleybus replacement route replacing a tram replacement route. (Alan Mortimer)

Leaving Colindale (CE) trolleybus depot in early Spring sunshine, Willesden garage's RTL1410 starts its journey to Borehamwood, Rossington Avenue on Route 52A. At this time Willesden was a totally Leyland shed. An inspector checks his paperwork, possibly for the correct departure time, although he may only be interested in the trolleybus operations. A.Owen to this day is a respected Jaguar car dealer, although the Singer marque had disappeared and the Jaguar XK150 outside looks a 'snip' at £865. The depot houses at least two trolleybuses although unfortunately by this time next year they would be gone and the depot no longer operational. (Ron Wellings)

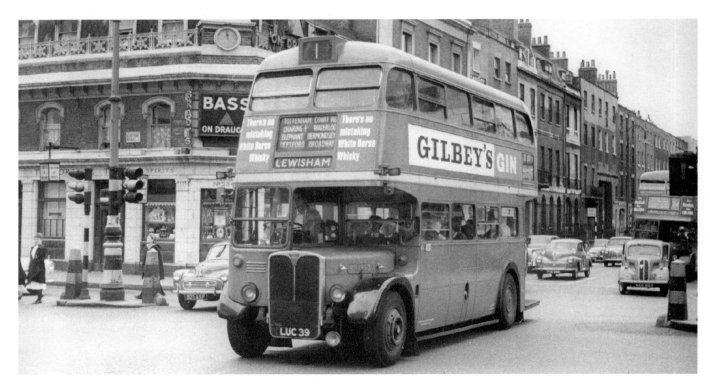

Nowadays Route 1 is but a shadow of its former self but in 1961 it still worked from Willesden and Marylebone to Lewisham. RT1953 heads across Euston Road in Gower Street, a move necessitated after 1st May when Tottenham Court Road became northbound only. Because right turns were prohibited in Euston Road, the 1 and 176 routes had to go north into Hampstead Road and reached Gower Street by way of Drummond Street. Pursued by a procession of cars including two Morris Minors, a Ford Popular and an Austin A30 it is followed up by an RTW on Route 24 making its way to Pimlico. The New Cross RT is running across the piece of road which will eventually be excavated to construct the Euston Road underpass. (Alan Mortimer)

Route 325A was a very shy creature introduced in 1958 providing one or two Monday to Friday peak journeys linking the Cottonmill Estate with Firbank Road at St.Albans rather than the New Greens Estate served by the parent route. On 7th June the 325A variant was withdrawn as part of the summer programme but before that RF543 is caught by the camera opposite St.Albans garage. (Ron Wellings)

The route number 243 was conveniently vacant when a number was required for the motorbus replacement of trolleybus routes 543 and 643 at stage 11 on 19th July. RM860 garaged at SF is seen at Stamford Hill as it journeys to Shoreditch, eschewing the Old Street, Clerkenwell Road section of the route on this particular duty. If the memory of my colleague is correct this bus was the first to venture out of Stamford Hill garage on Route N83 on the night of conversion. Experiments with the design of the grille to incorporate an AEC type triangle were in evidence at this time but not as yet in place on production vehicles. (Alan Mortimer)

This photograph just had to be included to highlight the extremes between a three wheel Heinkel (later Trojan) bubble car and an eight feet wide RTW bus. The car driver probably felt as safe pottering around the capital as the passengers on the number 45 bus but one has to wonder if he would be so happy today using this mode of transport. RTW76 traverses Pancras Road as it heads from Hampstead Heath to South Kensington Station, here covering the new extension north of the Thames introduced with the 9th stage of trolleybus replacement earlier in the month. The bus is one of the small number provided by Chalk Farm garage, Walworth providing the bulk of the route's scheduled mileage. (David Berwick)

New Cross garage appears to have had an attraction for green liveried vehicles when this print of trainers RT36 and RTL1275 is added to the other view of Green Line reliefs at the same location which appears in this volume. Neither 2RT2s or RTLs are usually associated with this colour scheme but small numbers of the former were repainted in 1955 for Country Area use at Hertford and some RTLs received green livery in 1959 for use at Hatfield. Neither of the two buses seen here returned to their more customary colour scheme before departing the Executive to go their separate ways in April 1963 and May 1964 respectively. (John Gascoine)

RM489 heads a line of trolleybuses which have effectively blocked off Maple Street at the Tottenham Court Road terminus of various routes. Trolleybuses on routes 627 and 629 are still in service which allows this picture to be dated sometime between 1st February when route 653 was repaced by motorbus 253 and 26th April of the year under review when electric powered vehicles disappeared from this road. (A.D.Packer)

Buses for two former Athol Street routes stand on 30th September in the doorway of their new home, the former trolleybus depot at Poplar. Newly overhauled RTL1565 is dressed for the Isle of Dogs route 56 with the garage destination of Poplar, Aberfeldy Street while former Athol Street RTL467 carries the display for the Blackwall Tunnel route 108A. (John Gascoine)

With just a little battering to the front nearside mudguard and a small amount of damage to the roof, this ex-STD looks in reasonably good exterior order considering it has completed around five years use in Sarajevo. The lifeguard has been removed, the platform transferred to the other side and all blind box apertures panelled over. Now carrying its new owner's fleet number 28 and Sarajevo identification in its registration number it is seen in its home city on 24th August. (D.Trevor Rowe)

In the last throes of wearing its Central Area colour scheme before losing it on overhaul in June when it was outshopped in Country Area green, RT4610 is seen on Route 25 at Aldgate Station en-route to Becontree Heath. It had arrived at West Ham garage along with sixty seven other RTs upon the closure of Forest Gate garage in April 1960 at which time the former trolleybus depot had first begun to operate this long established trunk route. (Alan Mortimer)

Former G267 is an unusual looking ex-London Transport Guy having been rebodied with a Croft lowheight 55 seat body to replace its original highbridge Massey example. Acquired by Western SMT of Kilmarnock in 1952 it received this second-hand structure the following year. It is seen on 5th June parked within the yard of Longtown garage near the end of its Scottish career which ended with its disposal to Milburn Motors of Glasgow. (J.G.E.Nye)

Punters and visitors are absorbed in making or losing money on the horse racing and only the bus photographer explores the bus and coach park at Ascot. With no interference green RT2157 with duty plates WR218 is recorded on the 443 service being one of Windsor's contributions on this race day. Regular operation on this route was withdrawn on 25th October but the number was retained for use on the special race day service. This bus had originally entered service in Central Area colours in April 1949 from Hounslow garage. Upon its second overhaul in July 1956 it was outshopped in the Country colour scheme to be garaged at Staines. Since then it has had a further overhaul and is now carrying body number 9193 of Weymann manufacture. Once one of the later members to join the preservation movement it sadly found itself as an immobile estate agent's office further in its course through life. (Alan Mortimer)

These sad and depressing views of TF class coaches, once the pride of a number of Green Line routes, were the scene which intrepid photographers were to encounter for a number of years at the Whinmoor premises of the dealers W.North. The view above shows TF30 with TF46 resting beside while the lower view is of TF76. All three vehicles show signs of having stood neglected and vandalised for many years. These 1939 coaches had been withdrawn from service by July 1953 and disposed of to W.North and these pictures date from July of the year under review. Thankfully one representative of the class, TF77, is preserved today but what a pity more could not have been achieved in the nineteen fifties given the longevity of these wrecks. (R.F.Mack (above))

Waiting to depart for Sevenoaks as a relief 705 shortly after its July overhaul, RT4407 garaged at Dunton Green is seen on Eccleston Bridge. The Green Line Coaches sign almost gives the impression that this roadway is an exclusive Green Line coach station. The chassis of this bus, now fitted with body number 2366, had first entered service in November 1953 carrying the red liveried body once mounted on SRT56 and numbered 4710. In May 1957 at the time of its first overhaul it was outshopped together with several others at the time in green livery primarily to replace Central Area examples then on loan to the Country Area. It was to keep its new basic green colour scheme for the rest of its public service use in London until disposal by London Country Bus Services Ltd. in July 1972. (W.R.Legg)

Still carrying body number 361 with which it had first entered service from Chelverton Road garage in April 1940, LPTB bodied RT58 was disposed of to Bird's Commercial Motors of Stratford Upon Avon in April 1960. It was then acquired by the Ayrshire Bus Owners (A1 Services) of Ardrossan and repainted into this superb paint scheme entering service soon afterwards. It was captured on film on 18th March of the year under review. Unfortunately being withdrawn in July 1962 it did not serve its new owners as long as they might have hoped for. Returning to Bird's in 1963 it was noted partially scrapped in 1965. (A.J.Douglas)

It was originally intended to convert trolleybus route 629 to bus operation in November 1961 along with the rest of Wood Green depot but the impending one-way system connected with the construction of the Euston Road underpass at Warren Street Station meant the conversion to motor bus 269 was brought forward to 26th April. One of the effects of this was the allocation of five Routemasters to West Green to assist with the Monday to Friday operation until November. Here one of them, RM754, crosses into Tottenham Court Road from Hampstead Road before the road works upheaval had begun. Chalk Farm's RTW14 passes, heading north on Route 24. (F.W.Ivey)

Harper Brothers of Heath Hayes acquired ex-RT1479 in July 1957 from Bird's Commercial Motors and gave the vehicle their fleet number 12. Neatly finished in the operator's green colour scheme, the front roof box has been retained although the offside route number plate holder has been removed. While the location of this photograph has not been established the bus appears to be awaiting departure on a journey to Kingstanding, a suburb to the north of Birmingham. (Alan Mortimer)

The trolleybus operation at Stamford Hill came to an end on 19th July of the year under review when the depot became a garage stocked entirely with the RM class of vehicle. These shiny new buses were initially for use on the 67 and 243 routes Mondays to Saturdays, 149 and 243A on Sundays and the all night route N83. Increased involvement with bus operation took place on 11th October when the 149 allocation changed to Mondays to Saturdays and a considerable daily allocation was introduced on service 253. RM801 pauses at Stamford Hill, having commenced its journey at Northumberland Park Station en-route for London Docks, Leman Street covering former trolleybus route 647 from this point south. (Alan Mortimer)

The five observation windows in the coving of the roof made the passenger saloon on the RW class very light and airy and was reminiscent of the private hire RFs. The rear emergency door on the offside behind the rear wheels and the sliding opening windows are departures from the style of the last single deck class put into service. RW3 waits for the driver/conductor with the Valley Hotel at Caterham as a backdrop before its departure for Reigate LT garage on Route 440. (Alan Mortimer)

After just over five years service with London Transport what was once RTL1494 found itself in the ownership of Walsall Corporation Transport as their number 205. First entering service from Chalk Farm garage in April 1954 it was allocated to CF until its only overhaul which took place in July 1957 when it emerged from Aldenham carrying Park Royal body number 4970 and re-entered service from Seven Kings. In December 1958 it was delicensed and removed to North Street, Romford garage for storage, eventually to be disposed directly to its new owners together with four other examples of the class in August 1959. Note the addition of a direction indicator low down beside the driver's door, a rather neater arrangement than the familiar London ears. (Alan Mortimer)

APPENDIX I

London Transport Central and Country Area Bus Garages

A	Sutton	K	Kingston
AB	Twickenham	L	Loughton
AC	Willesden	LH*	Leatherhead
AD	Palmers Green	LS*	Luton
AE	Hendon	M	Mortlake
AF	Chelverton Road, Putney	MA*	Amersham
AK	Streatham	MH	Muswell Hill
AL	Merton	N	Norwood
AM	Plumstead	NB	Norbiton
AP	Seven Kings	NF*	Northfleet
AR	Tottenham	NS	North Street, Romford
AV	Hounslow	NX	New Cross
AW	Abbey Wood	ON	Alperton
B	Battersea	PB	Potters Bar
BK	Barking	PM	Peckham
BN	Brixton	PR	Poplar
BW	Bow	Q	Camberwell
BX	Bexleyheath	R	Riverside
C	Athol Street, Poplar	RD	Hornchurch
CF	Chalk Farm	RE*	London Road, Romford
CM*	Chelsham	RG*	Reigate
CN	Carshalton	RL	Rye Lane
CS	Chiswick (non-operational)	S	Shepherds Bush
CT	Clapton	SA*	St.Albans
CY*	Crawley	SJ*	Swanley Junction
D	Dalston	SP	Sidcup
DG*	Dunton Green	ST*	Staines
DS*	Dorking	SV*	Stevenage
DT*	Dartford	SW	Stockwell
E	Enfield	T	Leyton
ED	Elmers End	TB	Bromley
EG*	East Grinstead	TC	Croydon
EP*	Epping	TG*	Tring
EW	Edgware	TH	Thornton Heath
GD*	Godstone	TL	Catford
GF*	Guildford	TW*	Tunbridge Wells
GM	Gillingham Street, Victoria	U	Upton Park
GR*	Garston	UX	Uxbridge
GY*	Grays	V	Turnham Green
H	Hackney	W	Cricklewood
HB	Hammersmith (BEA Coaches)	WD	Wandsworth
HD	Harrow Weald	WG	West Green
HE*	High Wycombe	WH	West Ham
HF*	Hatfield	WL	Walworth
HG*	Hertford	WR*	Windsor
HH*	Two Waters, Hemel Hempstead	WW	Walthamstow
HL	Hanwell	WY*	Addlestone
HT	Highgate (part trolleybus)	X	Middle Row
HW	Southall	-	Aldenham (non-operational)
J	Holloway		

* indicates a Country Area garage.

This is a list of garages as at 1st January 1961. With trolleybus conversion four new bus garages were added to the list during the year. These were:

EM   Edmonton (partially converted 26th April and fully 19th July).
FY   Finchley (partially converted 8th November).
SF   Stamford Hill (19th July)
WN   Wood Green (partially converted 26th April and fully 8th November).

In addition Highgate (HT) became fully converted on 26th April.

One garage closed during the year and that was Athol Street, Poplar (C). Its entire allocation of RTL buses and the two RFW coaches housed there were moved to Poplar (PR) on 10th May when work on the facilities there which had started in 1959 were finally completed.

APPENDIX II

A special thank you is extended to the following correspondents for their interest in providing helpful comments and information to either assist in updating or correcting captions in earlier titles in this series of books or in answering queries arising in the preparation of this present volume. Laurie Akehurst, Colin Bull, Alan B.Cross, Michael J.Burrow, C.Fitzgibbon, D.S.Giles, David Gover, Peter Gulland, Brian Harding, Henry Heyworth, Peter Holmes, Andrew G.Johnson, Barry Maynard-Smith, John W.Millbank, George Moon, Alan Munro, Lewis W.Norris, John Reynolds, John Smart, John G.S.Smith, David Stewart, James Stirling of 'Allsorts', Croxley Green, Michael R.B.Taylor, John Winteridge and Alan Wood.

1946 BOOK

Page 56   RT38 in the lower picture is parked in Allsop Place, NW1.

Page 106   T543c is actually traversing Allsop Place which is near Baker Street.

Page 109   It appears from a local contemporary correspondent that lowbridge STLs did not appear on Route 230 until December 1942 when partial conversion took place although the October date stated in the caption has often been quoted in other sources.

Page 112   I have been corrected on the length of time needed to accumulate enough coupons for a new top coat which was nearer seven months than seven years but still a long time to wait.

Page 115   ST988 is parked outside the then named Merton Road School in Merton Road, Southfields. The school, at the corner of Replingham Road was soon renamed Riversdale.

Page 121   T230 is on the stand in Belmont Road, Wallington which has not changed over the years except for new lampposts.

Page 122   XN1781 was twenty five years old when photographed in 1948, not forty five as stated in the caption.

1947 BOOK

Page 9   My sincere apologies to John W.Millbank who I inadvertently forgot to thank in the acknowledgements for the use of his work on pages 107 and 108.

Page 76   The caption is misleading as the bus is travelling towards Southfields, the conductor having already changed the blind for a return journey to Camden Town.

Page 83   EXF921 was a 1938 Leyland LZ chassis, no.200050, with Harrington coach body seating 32. It was new to Grey Green of London and appeared on some of their publicity at the time.

Page 97   Apologies are due since C42 is pictured outside 'The Tea Caddy' which was in Tring not Chesham as stated. This establishment was run by a well known local lady, Polly Perkins, who after finishing employment as a wartime 'clippie' opened the tea shop opposite the entrance to Tring garage.

Page 144   The Bull Yard, Peckham was of course the site used for the construction of Peckham (PM) garage, not Rye Lane (RL) as stated.

1948 BOOK

Page 47   ST383 in the top picture is seen in Middleton Road, St.Helier opposite the St.Helier Memorial Hall built in 1930 and still in use. The open site immediately behind the bus now houses the Meldrum Hall.

Page 64   In the lower picture ST716 is standing in Epsom Road, Morden, the trees in the background forming the boundary of Morden Park which nowadays is fenced.

Page 67   The UCOC Bristol, fleet number 653, is in Buckingham Palace Road, Victoria.

1950 BOOK

Page 28   In the top picture STL2284 is travelling south at the Epsom Clock Tower stop in Epsom Market Place.

Page 30   LT1129 is pictured in Elm Road, Hackbridge, the terminal now only used by buses on Route 151 turning short towards Wallington.

Page 32   Q150 in the lower picture is at the 'Worcester Park' public house opposite the Southern Region station.

Page 36   In the lower picture STL1493 is at the same location, Epsom Clock Tower, as STL2284 mentioned above.

1951 BOOK

Page 85   LT1024 is standing at the Elm Road, Hackbridge terminus.

Page 91   STL2311 is on the stand in Hardwicke Road, Reigate.

1952 BOOK

Page 7   C59 is at the Holland (Coldshott) terminus in Holland Road used by buses on Routes 464 and 465.

Page 155   In the top picture Q238 is standing at Guildford garage.

1953 BOOK

Page 27   T767 is in Brighton Road, Purley.

Page 42   In the lower picture the car parked behind D25 is a 1934/35 Humber 12h.p. Vogue saloon model.

Page 62   In the upper picture a 1952/53 Humber Super Snipe follows immediately behind RTL775.

Page 72   In the lower picture a Vauxhall 14h.p. J type saloon is parked alongside T789.

Page 116   The car parked at the kerbside behind RTL1373 is a 1933 Ford 8h.p. which is confirmed by the straight bumper of heavier section, shallow depth radiator and no wing skirts.

Page 149   An 'Oxford' taxicab follows RTL61 in the lower picture.

1954 BOOK

Page 138 The double ended blind has caused confusion. RTL1076 is heading for South Kensington having reached Onslow Square at the junction with Pelham Street. It will then embark on its one-way circuit to the terminal to pick up outside the station's northern entrance in Thurloe Street before departing for the Festival Gardens.

1955 BOOK

Page 18 RTL1065 is standing outside 9 Disraeli Road, Putney which has received much media attention of late as it now houses the Putney Conservative Association of David Mellor the ex-M.P. Why the F garaged bus has stopped here, short of the Oxford Road stand, is a mystery. Maybe the conductor had an overdue book to return to Putney Library which is behind the bus.

Page 21 RTL1356 in the top picture is standing beside the part of Battersea garage in Hester Road now used by Kentish Bus to operate Route 19.

Page 116 In the lower picture the buses on Routes 127 and 151 are outside Martell's the furnishers of 10-14 Stonecot Hill, opposite the 'Woodstock' public house.

1956 BOOK

Page 23 In the top picture a Standard Vanguard II follows RT1490.

Page 24 The bottom photograph is from the camera of the late Don Thompson. The withdrawal date in the caption gives the impression that the route was withdrawn in the year under review whereas it was in fact 20th August 1958.

Page 33 A Morris Minor II with body of the third major revision stands behind ex-B4 in the lower picture.

Page 59 Ex-TR29 was re-registered in May 1950 at the time it was rebodied with the Thurgood 35 seat coach body shown here and numbered 635.

Page 66 Red Rover's RT31 is at Waddesdon cross roads about half a mile south of the village on the A41 standing on the gravelled surface in front of the wrought iron gates of the least used entrance to Waddesdon Manor.

Page 90 Apologies to all the car enthusiasts who have pointed out that the car squeezing between the GS and a road bollard in the lower picture is a Standard 10 with a December 1954 registration, not a Vauxhall as stated.

Page 97 An Austin A70 Hereford car comes into view on the left hand side of the upper picture of ex-B25.

Page 123 In the lower picture ex-D272 is riding over the tram lines in Wellington Street, Leeds abandoned on 21st July 1956. The Leeds City Transport bus following is from the 1949/50 batch of all Leyland Titan PD2/1s numbered 340-399 and is working the 72 service from Bramley garage to Bradford jointly worked with Bradford City Transport.

Page 125 The bottom picture was taken in Britannia Street presumably on a Sunday while the crew were using the facilities offered at the Wellington Street coach station.

Page 143 A.H.Kearsey Ltd. were a Cheltenham based company running services to various Cotswold destinations as well as being involved in contract work. GT5099 carried fleet number 42 while in their ownership and was disposed of for scrap in September 1950.

The following photographs in this volume should be credited to Alan B.Cross: RT110 (page 29 lower); RT1517 (page 42 lower); Interior view of Stockwell garage (page 44 upper); RT319 (page 55 lower); RT1499 (page 65 lower); RT3958 (page 80 upper); RT114 (page 87 lower).